Thirteen women explore motherhood in this eloquent and moving book. Joy and fascination, uncertainty and ambivalence, run as common threads, as does the persistent grip of wanting to be the 'perfect mother'. There are recurring questions and a wide variety of responses. How do children change women's lives? Do you, must you, become another person when you have a child? How do women who care for children also look after their own needs and desires? Can we balance children and work? How do fathers engage in parenting? The circumstances in which these women bring up their children vary hugely, their pleasures and difficulties range over the whole gamut of experiences. Many speak of society's disregard for the needs of mothers, both over practical matters and deeper needs. This remarkably candid book tells us much about a state 'both more overwhelming and entrancing than I could have dreamed'.

Katherine Gieve, the editor of this collection, was born in Oxford in 1949 and grew up in Liverpool. After leaving university, where she read politics, philosophy and economics, she became involved in the women's movement, first with the women's lobby and then with the Campaign for Legal and Financial Independence. As a solicitor she has worked principally on family law and the legal implications of cohabitation and illegitimacy; on cases concerning children and local authorities and on law reform in that area. She writes freelance on both feminism and the law, and has co-authored the *Cohabitation Handbook* (Pluto Press). She lives in London with her husband and their two children.

BALANCING ACTS

On Being A Mother

Edited by
Katherine Gieve

VIRAGO

For Daniel and Matthew

Published by VIRAGO PRESS Limited 1989
20–23 Mandela Street, Camden Town, London NW1 0HQ

This collection and introduction copyright © Katherine Gieve
1989
Copyright © in each contribution held by the author 1989

A CIP catalogue record for this book is available from the British
Library

Typeset by Goodfellow & Egan Ltd, Cambridge
Printed in Great Britain by
Cox & Wyman Ltd, Reading

Contents

Acknowledgements   vi
Introduction   vii

Wanting It All   Helena Kennedy   1
In a Different Key   Elizabeth Wilson   11
Burning in the Cold   Yasmin Alibhai   24
And Not To Count the Cost   Katherine Gieve   41
The World Became a More Dangerous Place   Victoria Hardie   52
Girls Can't Be Professors, Mummy   Hilary Land   73
Giving Birth Again   Rahila Gupta   94
Very Much Part of the Experiment   Elizabeth Peretz   107
Joseph   Gillian Darley   123
My Pride and Joy   Jean Radford   132
Medea and Marmite Sandwiches   Jennifer Uglow   145
The Best of All Worlds?   Margaret Smith   160
Motherhood in the Imagination   Julia Vellacott   177

Biographies   204

Acknowledgements

I would like to thank all the contributors for writing these essays and for the great pleasure I have had in working with them. I would particularly like to thank Julia Vellacott for her help with the whole collection. In working on this book I have drawn on so many conversations and shared experiences that it would be impossible to list all those friends who have helped me. I am particularly grateful to Linda Dawson, Sybil del Strother, Rosie Parker and Paula Weideger for their helpful comments on the manuscripts, and to Ruthie Petrie at Virago who encouraged me to embark on this project and who has helped me to bring it to fruition.

My parents Charles and Patricia Vereker have given me continuous support and encouragement. I thank, too, my husband John Gieve, my sternest critic.

Introduction

Katherine Gieve

As I waited for the birth of my first child, I felt poised on the edge of the world. I wondered, will I be the same person? What sort of mother do I want to be, do I have any choice, and how can I fit being a mother into my pre-baby identity? The intentions which seemed quite clear and uncomplicated before birth were fraught with difficulties and ambiguities afterwards. After, looking back, that time seemed like a remote era of peace and reflection, another world.

I wanted to put together this collection of essays to explore the experience of motherhood: to understand better the contradictions between being a mother and maintaining some independence and a place in the outside world. In some ways to write about one's own life as a mother seems audacious, what meaning or significance can it have for other women, limited as the experience of each person is by age, class, race, and time? But aspects of motherhood are universal; not only do babies have the same needs but we are all in thrall to powerful images of motherhood. The way in which each woman grapples with the ideals and asserts and discovers her own identity is important for other women and can help to provide a framework for understanding the difficulties we live with. Elizabeth Wilson, writing about her own mother, describes her feelings about the 'depersonalising epithet of "mother" ', and the need to prize the particularity of her relationship to the child she cares for to whom she did not give birth. This is no less a need for those of us who have given birth: to keep a sense of ourselves as particular people in relation to our children and yet balance that with the need to satisfy our children and our own image of how we should be as mothers.

In a curious way, to be worthy of the description 'mother' you must be a good mother. For fathers it is different – a good father is quite different from merely a 'father'. And so when my first child was born his father was frequently congratulated on being a good father, on taking to it so well, while for me it seemed taken for granted as part of the job that I should adapt myself to circumstances which were no less novel. Nature is expected to come to the aid of women to transform themselves from individuals into ideals. Victoria Hardie writes, 'It is as though no one has ever been able to see their own mother as a human being, so great has been the cover-up of what most mothers really feel, need, and perceive.'

The insistent demand from outside that mothers shall be perfect and all-restoring may have a resonance for each of us; an echo of our own desire to make things perfect for our children and perhaps in doing so to make good the rift between our own experience and our dreams. That desire indeed may be part of the reason for wanting to have children: 'But the desire for motherhood is also about the past. It's the desire to relive my childhood with the mother I desired to have rather than the mother I actually had. Is it the lost child or the lost mother I want to regain?' (Jean Radford).

So a mother faces both external and internal pressures for certainty and perfection and must find a way of reconciling the ideals and fantasies with reality and her own character. In learning about this and its meaning both for ourselves and our children, we need to understand more of the needs of a child and the possibility of their satisfaction. Julia

Vellacott provides a framework for thinking about unconscious desires; with relief I read about Freud's view that the child's love for the mother is by definition insatiable.

The demands of caring for a baby and for a small child arouse in us deep feelings: both joyous and painful. These feelings bear a curiously ambiguous relation to our sense of our own power. The essays reveal diverse experiences. For some women the capacity to give sufficiently to satisfy a small baby has given them a great sense of strength. 'There is a deep relief and pleasure at finding myself able to give again and again – what's needed: bottles, changes, attention' (Jean Radford); 'I had no idea I could love that well, nor that I would find the patience to cope with the unremitting nature of it all.' (Gillian Darley). But I myself experienced responding to those needs as a sort of passivity, not a strength, however satisfying.

Side by side with the coping comes also the not coping: the anguish of a hungry baby's cry becomes your own anguish; the rejected sadness of a child excluded from a game is felt as your own rejection. 'Our feelings as infants can be rearoused at any time and are particularly strongly called forth by caring for a totally dependent infant.' (Julia Vellacott). So the experience of motherhood means strength and responsibility. It also means emotional vulnerability as we try to satisfy needs which inevitably cannot be entirely satisfied and we are open to our own infantile experiences.

Some women have written, in this collection, about their own mothers. There is no uniformity in their images: some reflect powerlessness and the economic vulnerability which motherhood can bring with it. 'I seemed to be aware at a very early age that my mother was vulnerable, because she depended on my father's approval for our survival.' (Victoria Hardie); 'My mother, forced – as it appeared to me then – to choose between husband and child, had chosen me; and loss of status, poverty and shame were the result.' (Elizabeth Wilson). In contrast Yasmin Alibhai says of her mother, who also supported her family single-handed, 'There was never a sense of conflict, no feeling of being drained, or her selfhood being flooded out by motherhood, it was a vital addition, an extension of her strength.' For Helena Kennedy, 'Mothering was big business in our home . . . My mother was proud and confident of her role and people came to her for advice.'

In my thinking I have come full circle. Security and financial independence for women are needed to provide a framework for the extreme experiences of motherhood – so that the inevitable emotional vulnerability is not matched by economic vulnerability. Yet there is still a question about the self and what motherhood means. Yasmin Alibhai echoes my own fears when she writes, 'People are afraid that if they extend and give themselves, the "me" in them will be diminished, or lose shape.' Writing of her own culture she goes on to say: 'this concept remains totally alien to me. Our inner world tells us that the more you give, the more you grow. There is no panic about the gradual erosion of the self through the giving of yourself to others. That is why having a child is seen as an extension of the self and not a reduction of it.' There is no doubt, for me, that having children is an enriching experience. It has been the most important in my life. Yet the words "richer and poorer" do not do justice to the contrasts. I may be more open to my own feelings and those of other people; more open to the needs of others – but perhaps less purposive and single-minded and, for the moment, less engaged with the public world. With a twist the kaleidoscope has created a new picture.

Many women who grew up in the 1950s and 1960s and started their working lives with the ground swell of the women's movement, whether part of it or not, have hoped to be able to have children and also to be their own persons, earn their own living and play a part in the public world. It does not seem too much to ask. Yet as things are now it is a great privilege to do so without exhaustion and desperation, and a sense of shortchanging one world or the other.

The ideals of the women's movement require great changes in the public world: a willingness to restructure work conditions for those with domestic responsibilities; a willingness to use collective resources to provide better care for children outside their homes; a willingness to provide an environment that is more friendly to those who look after children. Neither the political rhetoric nor the practice of the 1980s has shown this willingness. The opposite is true.

Yet individual women have struggled on – not trying to have their cake and eat it – but just to have independent lives and to care for their children. More benevolent changes in the public world would have made this task much easier, but practical arrangements are only part of the story. There are many contradictions to understand and come to terms with in coping with the emotional stresses of motherhood and reconciling them with the rest of life.

We are not blank pages when we become mothers, no more are our children blank pages when they are born. Our choices of how we live in relation to our children and what sorts of relationships we can form with them are constrained, not only by the limitations and unfriendliness of the outside world, but also by ourselves. Before the baby it is difficult to imagine the emotional complexity of the experience, and before the toddler, and before the school age child and it goes on and on, each new stage, each different child, arousing new feelings, requiring more thought. And each new experience has its effects (maybe takes its toll) on close relationships with other people; fathers, partners, friends, families.

This book does not pretend to be a survey: chance has played a part in the choice of authors, but the choice has not been altogether random. I have tried to seek out women who have lived in different ways, who have children of diverse ages and have different sorts of work. Some women have been willing to write about special difficulties and of great sadness. I have asked, in the main, women for whom writing is familiar, if not part of their work, since it seemed to me that we could better describe the complexities of the subject if the writing itself were not too much of an impediment. This kind of selection inevitably brings with it a certain bias; a group of women who are privileged, if you like, in the way they earn their living. I know, even so, that many of the contributors have not found it at all easy to write about their lives, which change day by day even as they are being written about. At times it seemed a heavy burden to propose, to ask women who were already engaged in a double shift of work and childcare to write about it as well. Telling the story of one's life as a mother means telling the story of the lives of children and perhaps a partner. Each of the authors has had to find a balance between privacy and revelation.

The aim of the collection is to describe the collision between ideas and experience and to provide, not only autobiographies, but also reflections; these elements come in different proportions in each of the essays. I asked each of the writers to have in mind a central theme: what is the meaning to the mother of being a mother; and how has it been possible to maintain an independence in the face of the powerful bond of motherhood. These questions have a very different significance in the context of different lives. Independence is as dust if a baby has died, perhaps impossible to envisage for the mother of a child who is disabled, and an unattainable luxury for many many women.

But those questions are crucial for many women: how do those who care for children also look after themselves? Do you, must you, become another person when you have a child, or care for one intimately? Becoming a mother has profound implications for a woman's identity.

London, September 1988

Helena Kennedy

© MELANIE FRIEND

Wanting It All

Mothering was big business in our home. My mother feels good about herself as a producer of babies and carer of children. We were filled with cod liver oil, free orange juice and syrup of figs. We were always free of nits, had good let-down hems on our clothes and sensible shoes. My mother was proud and confident of her role and people came to her for advice. The kitchen was always full of the children of neighbours and aunts, and, by the time of my adolescence, the children of my own older sisters. My mother has an ample bosom and a sense of rhythm which can reduce any infant to a coma within minutes. She knows nursery rhymes you have never heard and old wives' tales that would make your hair stand on end. She likes babies and little children and loses interest as they approach adolescence. I absorbed from her an overwhelming sense that childbirth was miraculous, that having children was at the core of being a woman. My education took me on a long journey away from her and the obligations instilled in me by a Catholic girlhood. I wanted independence as a woman which made my mother afraid for me and which she saw as a rejection of some of her beliefs, but I was left in no doubt that I, too, wanted children. I wanted the experience which had made her life so worthwhile and I wanted, like her, to be good at it.

I was 32 when I decided to have a baby. Having practised as a barrister for ten years, I felt sufficiently secure in my career to take some time out as well as shoulder the financial responsibility of a child. I approached my pregnancy with enthusiasm, felt well and exercised regularly. My partner of many years standing and a close woman friend were both going to be there at the planned active birth. I loved the whole business. I sailed about in a sea of good feeling; jurors gave me knowing looks and benevolent smiles, and judges constrained from doing battle with me.

The birth did not go according to plan. Floor cushions, ice packs and breathing routines were abandoned for forceps and stitches, but I was ecstatic with my little son. He suckled and gurgled and slept and I was filled with bovine contentment. My mother arrived to cast her eye over her twelfth grandchild. In our overwhelmingly female family, a boy had novelty value, and she fell for him. I won an approval which all the legal victories in the world would not have extracted from her and the success of my breast feeding was lauded in her Glasgow kitchen.

My return to work was relatively smooth. While I had planned that Keir should go to a nursery after my three months at home it only became clear to me after his arrival that babies responded well to a certain amount of consistency and calm. Motherhood fits in well with an established rhythm which my own legal practice does not have. One of the pleasures of work at the Bar is the movement from court to court, from trial to trial. Juries sometimes do not return verdicts until late in the day. On occasions you have to leave early in the morning to travel to a far-flung court. The nursery routine depends on prompt picking up in the evening and dropping the baby off in the morning. Keir's father is an actor and the nature of his work meant that he would not always be able to help at those times of day either. I fought off my class resistance to having a nanny, and Tina came to work. She is with us still and is the person who has made my working life possible. She is capable and loving, and I whisper gratitude to the gods that she entered my life.

There were changes in my existence, but none bore out the dire warnings we had heard about the effect of a child upon our lives. I no longer dallied in Chambers to swap anecdotes about monstrous judges but sped home eager for Keir's smell and his smile. But life as we knew it did not stop. We took him with us everywhere and he happily slept in his carry-cot under restaurant tables and at political meetings. I changed nappies while reading briefs, and shovelled in baby rice as I practised my jury speeches on him. I thought I had cracked this motherhood lark: little did I know.

My personal life fell apart when Keir was a year old. I functioned on automatic for a while and then threw myself even more energetically at my work. Keir was a continuing delight to me and I tried to give him as much of myself as possible. My separation from his father seemed without effect upon him then, but I grieved over what the loss might mean to him in years to come. With the help of Tina, and close friends, life developed a different shape. Keir would go to bed at eight and sleep through until eight the following morning. He was a pleasure and a painless task for baby-sitters, and I was able to see friends and work very hard without too much anguish. In time I met Iain. Marriage and having another child with him made for a much more demanding home life. The pleasure is considerable, but for the first time I felt the guilt about juggling time.

Again my pregnancy was sheer bliss. I feel happy inside my own body when I am pregnant. I feel very sensual and freed by the absence of contraception. Everything is mellower in pregnancy; maybe I give myself permission to be less driven. Clio's birth was a triumph in that labour lasted only two hours, but I still feel that I am not very good at giving birth. I do not just go with it. I think I resist the loss of control that I fear is involved, but the joy, the joy, always makes me want to do it again. And here was a girl, not "other" but like me, but please not like me. I can close my eyes and recreate the feeling of fullness, completeness. The waves of emotion as the scrap of life first snuffled at my breast. After each birth that feeling has remained with me for days and weeks before being suborned by practical mothering.

Even before Clio arrived, Keir became rather clingy and temperamental. He felt the wind of so much change in his little life, and having loved the attention of Iain before we married, he had reservations about his permanent presence. We had each sold our homes and bought a house together, but Keir occasionally wanted to know when Iain was going back to his own place.

At first, Keir was delighted with his sister, but soon his deep misery became apparent. He expressed his feelings with great candour. He wanted to know if I was cross with him. There had to be some reason for my going off and having another baby. He thought it might be nice if Iain moved out and took Clio with him for company. Then his own daddy could come and look after him. He planned different combinations, all involving exile for the new arrival. He bore down on her from a height and called it a kiss. He squeezed her until she was puce in the name of a hug and sometimes he abandoned all guile and just thumped her or me. He felt utterly betrayed and did not attempt to hide his anger. He said he wanted Tina as his mummy and would cry for her when she left in the early evening. If only I could give an account of myself as the calm solicitous mother, reassuring this three-and-a-half-year-old with soothing words. I did sometimes manage it, but there were times when I wanted to throttle him.

My patience was most sorely tried first thing in the morning when he refused the breakfast which yesterday had been his favourite, when he forebore all sweaters, when he insisted that the elastic in his trousers hurt and wanted to wear plimsolls in the snow. My angel son, who had smiled his way through infancy, turned into a monster. He lay on the floor and screamed with rage, and I wanted to do the same. In fairness to us both, I should explain that Clio was no slouch at screaming herself. She had started screaming shortly after her birth and had only occasionally stopped for a breather. It seemed to get her a lot of attention, so why not the rest of us!

I saw a glint in the eyes of friends as they told me THIS WAS MOTHERHOOD. That idyll with Keir in his babyhood was not motherhood, all that coping happily. Now, they said, I was finding out what it was really all about.

I have little recollection of those early months of Clio's life; it has become a blur with an aching tiredness as its main theme. She cried constantly, rarely slept, and fed in a desultory way. I was suddenly much less confident of my own ability as a mother. I felt I was out of tune with whatever she needed and believed my success with Keir was only due to his good nature. I could not accept that it was just that my two children were very different. I was convinced that if I had ever had any nurturing skill, it was clearly inadequate. Leave her to cry, or keep her with you, supplement with a bottle, persist with the breast. It's wind, it's colic, it's an immature digestive system! Try gripe water, camomile, massage, homeopathy! Is it any wonder Keir was miserable too. I guiltily relished the idea of escaping into my work.

Just at the time of Clio's birth, I had been offered an opportunity that was new and exciting and one I was desperate not to miss. The producer of BBC's 'Heart of

Matter' had approached me about presenting the programme for two series. I had already been involved in a number of television programmes around legal issues, but this was a new departure and would mean learning a lot about the medium with very professional and skilled people. I liked the producer enormously and knew we would make a good team. She also appreciated the special problems I would have as a mother and wanted to accommodate them as much as possible within the limits of a big corporation. Once I had made the contractual commitment, I did not want to let her down.

As I expected, working on the programme was demanding but wonderful. The sad part was that while Clio's sleeplessness continued, her days were just becoming sunnier as I started the job. I was hardly sleeping at night, but I wanted to keep my breast feeding going at that end of the day. It was my way of clinging to this idea of myself as 'big mamma'. I carted breast pumps around when I went off to interview bishops, and prolonged filming meant painful engorgement, but I persisted stubbornly. The hard part was not the week days or, as the series progressed, the time spent away during the week, but having to work through the weekends. That is our one opportunity to all be together, particularly since Iain is a hospital doctor working long hours. Although the schedule meant I had a slacker time at the beginning of the week, that was no substitute to Iain who was working, or to Keir who was at nursery school.

For the first time I began to experience guilt, which I had never known when Keir was smaller. Clio had settled down now and I felt that I had not had any time to enjoy her. A calmness had descended on her and I was hardly there to take pleasure in it. Iain felt the lack of me, and Keir too was able to articulate his wants. The arrival of Clio heightened Keir's sense of having a different father. He suddenly spoke more about his own father as 'my daddy' as distinct from Iain, who was Clio's father. Today, most of the time he is content to explain to his friends that he has two daddies, but whenever he is sad he raises the idea of his father, him and me being all together as it is in the books. Anything else that is wrong for him I can try to put right, but that simple request leaves me wretched. It feels then as though I have found my happiness at the expense of his.

I had always felt so disturbed by the exhibitions of macho mothering I had overheard in robing rooms at the Bar where women vied with each other over how little time they took off to have babies, and bragged about nannies doing night feeds and about shunting their children off to boarding schools as soon as possible. I used to wonder why they had children at all. Yet here I was, losing out on that precious time. I felt the conflict of my own desire to work and to be with my children. I knew I wanted both. Having two children had meant the paring down of commitments. I had eliminated evening and weekend meetings, and had to take a much lesser role in the running of Chambers. Publicly at the Bar, I had never allowed problems with the children or child care to be used as an excuse for anything, although I had said to my clerks that I was not prepared to be away from home on a case for more than a day or two. It meant I had been unable to do any of the miners' riot cases and other important trials.

Women with children, I realised, compartmentalise their domestic and public lives. The unspoken rule is never to mix the two, or invoke one in aid of the other. The image of the capable woman must never be tainted by the smell of baby powder; efficient women have that side of their lives well under control. Motherhood is like some skeleton kept in the cupboard and most of us collaborate in keeping our children invisible. We have the terrible fear that to concede that there are emotional pulls or practical complications will be used against us. In the legal profession, it is certainly more acceptable for a male counsel to explain his late arrival because of a car breakdown than it is for a woman counsel to invoke the illness of her children's nanny. Most judges are men of an older generation who feel that the mothers of young children should not leave them anyway. Women therefore disguise the occasional hiccup in their domestic arrangements with the same broken-down-car excuse as their male colleagues.

Recently, in a case in the Coroner's Court, one barrister asked the Court to rise early so that he could keep a pre-arranged appointment in connection with his legal practice. The Coroner was happy to oblige, but asked us all if we would sit at 8.30 a.m. the following day to catch up on lost time. I explained that as the mother of two young children, I could not easily re-arrange my childcare at such short notice. The Court sat at the usual time, but not without a lot of sighing and asides from Court staff about working mothers and our part in the degeneration of society.

When I was making a programme about women on and in television, women presenters and producers with children all talked about these problems. If your children were a consideration, it was felt you were not giving yourself 100 per cent to the job. The very lack of structure and flexibility of television's working hours can be a disruption rather than a boon to women with children. Knocking ideas around, rattling a scheme for a programme until it feels right, are part of the business, and this most readily happens over a drink at the end of the day's work. To be unavailable then is to be excluded from an important part of the creative process. As with the criminal trial, nothing is more important than the job in hand and when just one more hour's filming might achieve the perfect interview, when just one more rejig of some footage might clarify an issue, it is an almighty drag to insist on pushing off home to read bed-time stories. You feel you are being unsupportive even to mention it.

Correspondingly, if some languorous time is not spent with your children at the end of the day, their real preoccupations and thoughts are never heard. It is only when you are in the bath or bed together, or immersed in a game of tiddly winks or a story, that you are asked if God is make-believe or why Daddy is not visiting us, or when we are going to die or why you cannot be seven straight after being four. What they all want is time for themselves, and you have to really listen without the back of your brain rehearsing legal arguments or cross-examination or without being seduced away by the telephone. One of my close women friends told me I was not very good at 'pottering'. I laughed! When was there time to potter? The energy with which I pursue a job permeated everything I did, yet it is in those idling times that the best communication often takes place. Compulsory pottering is the new regime.

By the end of Clio's first year, I was having to take stock. A month of holiday together in the summer had been glorious. The difference in temperament of my children, which had thrown me in Clio's early months, became a source of delight and bemusement. Clio's energy and determination had her walking by eleven months and shouting clear words soon after. She still wakens twice in the night, but with great charm will accept a drink and then snuggle down. She looks like an imp with her vivid blue eyes. My mother-in-law thinks she is plain and says she looks like me! I think she is glorious. She too wants stories read and games to be played. She too wants time exclusively for her.

Keir emerged from his jealousy bold and playful and full of touching warmth for his sister who was no longer so boring and wretchedly tearful. She had become an adoring witness to his daring exploits, a willing spear carrier in all his imaginative dramas and the most generous audience for his jokes. He responded with tender protectiveness and immense patience towards her disruptive efforts. He recovered his own equilibrium and confidence and feels good about the world again. His anger with me has also melted and I have been forgiven my treachery in introducing Iain and Clio into our blissful togetherness.

The Bar plus children was workable. The Bar and the children and the rigorous time frame of a series like 'Heart of the Matter' was not. Something would suffer and I could not risk it being our life at home. With grieving and gnashing of teeth, I stepped out of the BBC.

I know that I cannot be a full-time mother at home. I become restless and impatient and crave the outside world, but when at the other end of the spectrum I am working full-tilt, juggling jobs and selling the children short of time, I become tense and think I am failing them as a mother. All my rational being confirms the rightness of my wanting to work in a demanding area of the law. In the span of my life the infancy of my children is short, but to withdraw completely from work would be for me unfulfilling and would inevitably retard the development of my career. I know that the law will never do justice to women if progressive women are not in there fighting our corner, but in some hidden recess of my heart, I feel I am greedily wanting it all. By having a partner, children and exciting work, I am laying claim to more than I deserve. I am haunted by the privilege I enjoy as a professional woman who is paid well to do what I love doing. Some Catholic weighing scale in my inner recesses tells me that a price will be exacted.

I still fantasise about being the perfect mother. I save old bones at the back of the fridge in the vague hope of making stock and cock-a-leekie soup like my mother's. I hoard egg cartons and bottle tops for inspired artwork with my offspring. I bake the birthday cake in the shape of Thomas the Tank Engine; all we need is a bit of soft focus on the lens and I am as good as any of those mothers in the television ads.

Elizabeth Wilson

In a Different Key

I grew up with my mother in the drab 1940s: austerity and rationing, rising damp and dry rot, queues and fuel shortages suffused our relationship with a gloom that seemed eventually to pertain to motherhood itself. My mother's personality, her very identity, seemed to have been lost in domestic drudgery. The struggle with power cuts and ration books was somehow due to her having been 'deserted' by my father; and in some obscure way I was to blame. My mother, forced – as it appeared to me then – to choose between husband and child, had chosen me; and loss of status, poverty and shame were the result. She had no identity except that of mother; not a wife, not a worker, just a slave. A dark image of the feminine destiny insensibly engraved itself on my mind, although in retrospect it was her role as dutiful daughter, caring for elderly parents from whom she never broke free, that was at least partly responsible for her marginal, oppressed existence.

I can clearly remember thinking, as I crossed a bomb site on my way to school one day: 'I don't want to be like her when I grow up.' Surely at that period was formed an unconscious conviction that I was not going to have children myself, or rather, was not going to become a mother; but it was never a deliberate decision. By the time I had left university I had worked out a position (based on a superficial understanding of existentialism) of bohemian rejection of woman's expected role, and wrote to my mother to explain my intention never to marry. Predictably, she was horrified – no doubt this was intended, although I was too absorbed in my role as the Simone de Beauvoir of West London to calculate consciously my effect on her. My indifference to her feelings was all part of our grudging, withholding relationship. But in any case she was bound to be horrified, for, like many women whose marriages have proved unhappy, and whose children have been ungrateful or unforgiving, she could imagine no other destiny for me than to repeat the song, but in a major, not a minor key, she was to live the story again through me, only this version was to be the one with the happy ending. As she used to say with satisfaction of a film or novel: 'It all came right in the end.'

Yet my rebellion was not against motherhood or children as such. I was no career woman – indeed, that was another stereotype against which I fought – nor did I ever choose childlessness. I simply never thought through the issue of children, never thought much about children at all, I was simply against *marriage*. And despite today's myth of the 1960s as an era of freedom and permissiveness, it was almost unthinkable then to have children outside marriage. There was much more stigma, perhaps especially for middle-class women, in single parenthood than there is today.

Having lived out a form of 'freedom' outside the family in the 1960s, I came to women's liberation in the 1970s with a different set of experiences and expectations from many – perhaps most – of the women who made the early women's movement what it was. In fact, when I first heard about women's liberation I was not impressed. It sounded to me like a lot of heterosexual women whingeing on about a situation they themselves had chosen. They hadn't had to get married and have children. What did they expect? It was their choice, so why were they moaning? As a lesbian I felt that the stigmatisation and denigration I suffered was much more unjust, and it loomed much larger for me. Although I did not, of course, feel I'd been 'born that way', it didn't seem quite like a choice either; more like a romantic, slightly doomed destiny.

It didn't occur to me that possibly many of my contemporaries felt the same way about their (heterosexual) destiny. Recently, Claire Tomalin has written of Sylvia Plath's marriage to her fellow poet Ted Hughes, 'the Hughes, like many of us in that generation, had a vision of a Lawrentian marriage . . . in which the man would assert some primal sexual authority, while the wife submitted gloriously'.[1] It is my memory also that heterosexual love *was* perceived in this Lawrentian way then; and this heterosexual love ethic was one of the preconditions for the women's movement.[2] So for my contemporaries too, it was not exactly a question of choice. They had not really 'chosen' marriage and motherhood. For them heterosexuality may have seemed like an inescapable and glorious destiny (even if it later turned sour) just as lesbianism seemed a darkly glamorous, yet socially negated, destiny for me.

In any case, the whole false notion of 'choice' is inadequate when we discuss issues as intensely felt as sexual love and having children. The concept − false itself − of 'free choice' sets a false parameter of rationality around decisions the motivation for which may often be obscure. (This is so for abortion, as well, and although I believe it to be politically necessary, indeed vitally important, to argue for women's 'right to choose', the decision to have or not to have a child is probably never a wholly rational one.)

Within the early women's liberation movement motherhood seemed as problematic as it was in the world at large. The first feminist mothers I encountered lived in a collective household. Their alien paraphernalia of buggies and babygrows astonished me (I had imagined that babies were still going about in Silver Cross prams and hand-knitted layettes) and I found their maternal moodiness exasperating. I remember one hot summer day when they tried to invade the Ladies Pond on Hampstead Heath, where infants are strictly forbidden on grounds of safety − for the ponds are very deep. I was thoroughly glad that the place was free of tiresome children and bawling babies, and had no sympathy for the frustration of my new acquaintances, excluded from this feminist paradise, and complaining that children were never allowed anywhere, that public space denied their existence. They were right, of course, but oh, how irritating they were. They dragged about with louring expressions, always in the depths of some unalterable sense of grievance; they were, as we used to say then, 'heavy'.

Yet in principle I was always in favour of feminists having children. Socialists even more so; our numbers were so small, we must reproduce ourselves. I never felt, despite my earlier identification with Simone de Beauvoir, that the refusal of motherhood was a feminist solution to women's oppression, for surely that would be to go back to an old

14

stereotype of career woman versus wife, which seemed to me to belong to the 1930s rather than to the 1970s.

The concept of choice was wrong here too. In the 1950s and 1960s the sociologists had told us that women did now have choice – to work or not, to have children or not. But that was always a lie. Social pressures told another tale. On the other hand, by the 1970s feminists were not in any case arguing for choice. We wanted to create the conditions in which women could both undertake paid work *and* be mothers. The socialisation of housework, paid maternity leave, proper collective childcare, publicly funded, and decently paid jobs with shorter working hours were the solutions then advanced. And, however utopian they now sound, these still seem to me the only solutions. They came out of a vision of a cooperative and egalitarian order which in turn grew out of the experience of the women who came together at the beginning of the women's movement in 1970. Many of these women had had children in the isolating circumstances which prevailed in the 1960s: they came to the women's movement to find a way out of that isolation and inequality. They did not reject motherhood; they did demand that the conditions of motherhood should change.

Later in the seventies, however, their demands were reinterpreted. I was taken aback to realise that many of the younger women coming into the women's movement from the mid seventies onwards perceived my childlessness as some kind of feminist choice. They seemed also often to assume that feminism was saying that to be childless was the *only* feminist position, the only way of being a feminist. There was a misinterpretation of the experience of the early women's liberation movement; ironically, the distortions of the media appeared to be accepted by some younger feminists as a truth about feminism. Demands such as freely available abortion and twenty-four-hour nurseries were seen as an attack on motherhood itself, rather than as demands (not always well expressed, it is true) for the social

15

conditions in which women could have a different kind of choice — could choose positively to have children without giving up their place in the labour market or becoming wholly dependent upon a man, economically. The demand for twenty-four-hour nurseries, for example, was not intended to imply that mothers would abandon their children in residential care; it simply meant that childcare should be available for those working unsocial hours, in order to avoid the situation of families in which the partners virtually never met, because when one parent was at work the other was at home looking after the children, and vice versa.

Somewhere along the way, however, in the seventies, the rejection of the existing social circumstances of motherhood did get translated into a rejection of motherhood in any circumstances. As recently as 1986 Jenny Lecoat, the comedian, appeared on the Channel Four 'Comment' slot to 'confess' to a maternal feeling as she passed Mothercare. She, an independent, autonomous woman, had actually succumbed to a maternal pang! How terrible! How appalling! Even if this was slightly tongue in cheek (although it didn't come across as though it were) the assumptions were there — and in an unpleasantly bitter and self-hating form.

But then, towards the 1980s, as these younger feminists felt time running out, *their* decision to have 'late' babies could in turn be misinterpreted as a retreat. Hadn't these women after all — or so the popular interpretation went — tried to live without 'normal' love only to discover that nature can't be denied, that there are biological urges we ignore at our peril? This was a deeply conservative message; positioning women's independence on the one hand, and their fulfilment as mothers on the other (and this could include the longing for heterosexual love as well) as eternally in opposition. Both can never be achieved is the message: there is indeed a choice — on the one hand love and life, on the other the aridity of merely economic or intellectual existence.

The ideals of the early women's movement were other. What was to be done away with was not love, sexuality and relationships, but the coercion of unequal relationships between men and women. And we perceived – I still believe correctly – that women had to have economic independence if they were to lead emotionally satisfying lives as well. The position worked out by socialist feminists was a complex one, but it was not contradictory. We wanted men to be more involved in the care of children and in domestic work; but we wanted to unyoke these components of modern family life from the economic dependence of women on men on the one hand and – perhaps more controversially – from monogamy on the other. A mother might stay at home if she wished, but this should not be the norm. In a sense, we took 'choice' seriously.

The situation for the majority of women in Britain today has, if anything, deteriorated since the early seventies. They must juggle part-time, low-paid work with domestic responsibilities often shouldered alone. Today, feminism seems increasingly to mean a few highly paid women, driven and under stress, with nannies and domestic servants (although still not with husbands who share equally in domestic responsibilities), and a majority of women (including the vast majority of black women) in casualised, rock-bottom jobs. For women the class gulf is widening. Perhaps this is what 'post feminism' means. It is, for sure, not what we had in mind in 1971. But there it is. A few better educated, better trained women have been able to improve their position in the labour market, to postpone motherhood until in a relatively secure employment position, and to buy in childcare in the absence of public provision. The other side of this coin is the growing number of young women to provide these domestic services, owing to the lack of alternative employment, or because they themselves are single parents.

While motherhood in general was downplayed in the feminism of the 1970s, the lesbian mother became more visible. At first she was usually a woman who had been

17

married, but who had left her husband and 'come out'. Her problem was custody, and lesbians were and remain vulnerable in the Courts, seen as bad mothers, even as child molesters, although of course, ironically, children in a lesbian home are very much less likely to be sexually abused than children in a heterosexual or 'normal' home. Yet the presence of a father or father figure is still seen by judges, lawyers and social workers as better for the child than the home lacking patriarchal authority.

A small, but growing, number of women chose a different route to maternity: that of impregnation by artificial insemination. Clearly, there are drawbacks for the child: her 'fantasy father' can never be matched against reality, and may lead to an over-romanticisation of men, or to some gnawing sense of loss and mystery. For a woman to choose this method of becoming pregnant is sometimes interpreted as a total rejection of men at every level, and may therefore appear extremely threatening. Yet of course the whole process depends on the willingness of men to donate sperm. I see it not as an ideological statement, but simply as a practical option for women who long for a child, but who, for whatever reason, happen not to be in a sexual relationship with a man.

In 1984 the woman I live with had a baby by this method, and so, in the end, and to my own surprise I *have* become a 'mother' after all. For many women who struggle to bring up two or more children, isolated in the home and contending with an unhelpful husband, perhaps, it may seem that I am merely playing at motherhood. Others may regret on my behalf that I have not had the 'whole' experience. Everyone I know has been supportive and positive, including my partner's family and the local authority childminders and nursery workers, so we have so far been shielded from the hostility so often meted out to lesbian parents.

Yet, just as I'd felt alienated by the assumptions of those

feminists who assumed that I'd deliberately chosen not to have children, so in this new situation I found that the responses of other women, although not alienating in the same way, still failed to match my actual feelings. Now, many feminists were having babies in their thirties, 'after all'. (As one woman said to me, 'I *agonised* over this decision, only to find that I was just part of a trend!') So it was now assumed that this development in my life must be what I had 'really' wanted all along. 'Perhaps if you'd found out sooner you like children so much, you'd have had children of your own,' said a colleague. Yet I don't think that's true either. Once again, I didn't really choose, but simply went along with what my partner wanted. It is still true that the decision to have or not to have children has never set the terms for my life. Motherhood in the abstract still does not interest me that much, nor does the abstract idea of children. But children, of course, are individuals. Both in society at large and in the women's movement motherhood has usually been discussed in general, abstract terms, and the differences between one child and another, and the uniqueness of each mother's relationship to *her* child played down. And just as each child is an individual, so in my case it feels as if it is the child herself as much as anyone who defines the relationship, and this changes over time. This may seem painfully obvious, but it is the obvious that is not stated in a relationship overdetermined by ideology. For lesbian mothers and co-parents tend to be perceived from the outside either as monstrosities (by the world at large), or else (by the women's movement) transformed into heroines, ideologically correct and right-on women. But really we're just ordinary.

To begin with we cared for our child equally. (She had to be bottle fed, which for me at least was a plus.) At that early stage, despite the biological tie between mother and baby, when the baby still seems to the mother very much a part of herself, the infant's own undifferentiated response not only makes joint care easier but is functional for her, for her relatively indiscriminate smiles and coos attach adults to her at a time when both she and her mother are most vulnerable.

During the period at which most infants show their closest attachment to a single figure, we were living in the United States, where I was teaching, while my friend, still on maternity leave, became a housebound Californian housewife. This period was sometimes anomalous and uncomfortable for us both, despite the graciousness of Californians, in the Bay Area at least, where a lesbian couple with a baby is an accepted feature of the social scene.

When the child went to nursery at the age of two, she noticed much more that other children have fathers, for the first time asked questions, and for a while seemed upset, and sometimes angry with me. We must have been able to explain her situation in some way that satisfied her, and the subject receded in importance, but recently, aged nearly four, she has started to refer to it again, and has struggled to understand and define it for herself. Now, too, she has to cope with the questions of other children – although they have not yet learnt to be hostile or jeering.

What I have found so striking is the grace and sensitivity with which she deals with what must be sometimes painful or at least embarrassing for her. 'You're my friend, we are friends, Elizabeth,' she said to me, and actually I would much rather be a friend than an aunt, a father or a grandmother, roles that other adults have cast me in from time to time, for I resent the way in which everything has to be dragooned within the moral enterprise of the family, so that the only way adults have of showing their approval is to assimilate us to the nuclear family. This is understandable, but not really satisfactory.

In one way the situation is unusual. Yet the situation of a non-biologically related adult caring for a child has come to be so unusual only in recent times, in this country. In times past, and in other societies, children have often – whether by choice or by necessity – been cared for either by kin who

20

were not actual parents, or by non-kin. It is only today that the parental tie is given such over-riding importance, and is sanctioned by the state to the detriment of other relationships or arrangements, which wither into inadequacy by comparison. Yet, ironically, the family can be a dangerous place for both women and children. Soon after my return from the United States I attended an evening of readings by lesbian writers. The first contribution was an 'Open Letter' from a lesbian co-parent to her child. The letter dwelt on the difficulties of the relationship, among these being the indeterminate, undefined nature of the bond, marginalised by being outside the regulation of the State or even social custom. Thus, the writer argued, it was vulnerable, amorphous, unspoken.

Yet, as I listened, I could not help feeling that this was ironic, coming from a lesbian feminist, when one of the most serious points made by feminists about the position of women has been that the modern state is far too active in intervening in women's lives and defining their relationships in narrow and deeply oppressive ways. Perhaps there is some benefit to be derived from the existence of a relationship for which there is little definition, in which the roles are not prescribed in advance. And surely one of the lessons to be learned from the recent surge of women's writing, especially the writing of black women, of disabled women and of lesbians, is that the marginal can twist a source of strength out of their very marginality, that it is that marginality which gives their (our) view of the world a certain integrity. Simply because we have less of a stake in 'the system' we see it more clearly for what it is.

For all the discussion and writing about the personal being political, it is difficult to be completely true to one's experience, to reach what Keats called the truth of feeling (nor am I convinced that feelings always represent the deepest truth). Moreover both motherhood and lesbianism are so overlaid with stereotype that 'truth' is suffocated beneath an avalanche of preconceptions. How hard it is for us to see our mothers as anything other than 'mother' – a blank and blanketing word that covers over the individuality of the woman.

My grandmother used to assure me that my mother had wanted more children, especially boys, and for years I accepted this 'truth'. Yet, as a psychoanalyst helped me to 'see' for the first time, my parents were married for eight years without producing a child, and when I was less than a year old they left me with my grandmother and returned to Africa. During the dreary days of postwar austerity my mother used to reminisce endlessly about her wonderful pre-war life 'out in the tropics' – effectively when she was free of me. 'Out in the tropics' appeared as a heavenly, enchanted kingdom (in fact of course, it was the British Empire) from which she was now forever shut out.

So wasn't the truth of her feelings, perhaps, other than I'd always imagined? One evening in 1983 we went to the cinema to see *Heat and Dust*, a film about the British Raj. The heroine, a young British woman, married to a conventional civil servant (just like my father) falls in love and eventually runs away with an Indian prince, played by Shashi Kapoor. As we strolled out afterwards into the warm evening sunshine, my mother was ecstatic, but indignant too.

'We had such a *wonderful* time out there – it was all such marvellous fun. But what a stick the man was. They weren't like that at all, the young men, not one bit.'

I said nothing, not wanting to harp, for once, on the guilt about the British Empire she ought to feel, but didn't.

'Anyway, *he* was wonderful, wasn't he, the prince I mean, what a *marvellous* man –'

So, after all, she could, usually so predictable, surprise me. Suddenly she was a new person, a young woman carried away by the romantic Indian actor, and with the memory of those heavenly times, of her young womanhood before she ever became the dreary mother I had known (however lovingly wrapped up in me).

22

I am glad I met that vivacious young woman, even if only so briefly, before it was too late. For, only moments later, it seemed – only months at least – when my back was turned, the iron door of death slid down between us and she was gone. When I had not known her – had hardly known, after all, the woman beneath the stereotype, masked as she had always been for me by the depersonalising epithet of 'mother'.

I thought of her again, in California, as I pushed the baby round the dreaming suburbs. The heat was so brilliant that it whitened the grass and the air melted in the middle distance. In the midday silence we sat in the shade of a eucalyptus tree, and somehow, as the baby laughed and stretched out her hands towards a shaft of light I had a sudden, strong sense of my mother's identification with me. I was both baby and mother, and it was as if I lived for a moment in that happy time before she left me, in that eternal summer 'before the war'.

Notes

1. Claire Tomalin, the *Observer*, 6 March 1988, p. 43.
2. Elizabeth Wilson, *Only Halfway to Paradise: Women in Postwar Britain, 1945–1968*, Tavistock, London, 1980.

Burning in the Cold

As I began to drill into my soul, to examine my feelings about being a mother, a central question emerged out of this private excavation; what are the feelings of a feminist (of sorts), black Asian mother who has a male child in a racist country? It is a question that has racked me for ten years.

But before I can even begin to explore this profound question, I have something to say to all those white British women who will be reading this book. It is, in fact a long drawn out silent scream, full of fatigue and irritation, which you must now listen to.

Your ancestors and mine have had a relationship – albeit exploitative on one side – for generations now. And yet you do not know me and mine with any depth at all. Many of us interested in this subject, will, I suspect, be women of the same generation. Women, who through shattering world changes have created and coped with unique opportunities and responsibilities. We have had to live, too, with the frustration of finding out that when we thought we were running and well away, we were only running on the spot.

But these common experiences have not linked us in the way they might have done because they have been embedded in global power relationships and assumptions of white supremacy, which have informed the women's movement as much as anything else.

We therefore cannot have any real discourse about these changes, because in an ironic repetition of past patterns, things once more have been so one-sided, we have not evolved composite concepts, a language in common, or status equality which are the prerequisites for genuine understanding. Let me explain. I can discuss the finer points of any aspect of your cultural and social world with you, from George Eliot to George Harrison. Even though I can never belong to it, this world has vibrated in the background of my entire life. Yet you hardly know my world, and the little you have gleaned, you have harnessed to various causes and used. Much of the most forceful actions against domestic violence, for example, have been instigated by young Asian women. This has rarely been acknowledged in the women's movement. But it has always been remarkably easy for white women to seize upon what they perceive to be the complete oppression of Asian women in the home as an example of male brutality. Both these responses indicate how little you really know of our lives. By knowing so little, you are constantly surprised at finding out a little bit more. But without the build-up that comes out of a sustained interest and hard work, without that solid bedrock of assumed knowledge, all you can do is take tentative looks at something you really need to get your teeth into.

Unlike most of you, therefore, who will be reading or writing in this book, I cannot discuss anything personal or philosophical without telling you of my world, past and present. I cannot take anything for granted, and it is depressing that even my basic maternal feelings cannot be described without laying out the backdrop of my life, giving exact ingredients and measurements. How much more difficult then to describe the more abstruse thoughts and sentiments. The tedium of this fills me with apprehension. It is like writing out the etymology of all the words used in a poem before writing the poem. It strikes the poem and the spirit dead.

When it comes to feminist groups, the magic circles have been similarly exclusive. Their theories have often (not always) seemed strangely alien to the central impulses of my life as a mother and a woman, their struggles located in areas which often do not seem to make much sense to me. You would not be able to tell this because I speak your language and perform your rituals to finely tuned perfection, and can hold my own if necessary. But inside, I have felt uncomfortable and afraid that I would be exposed for not being a 'real' feminist because I have had these doubts.

I am not taking a cheap swipe at the women's movement, nor is this an idiosyncratic view. I know it is one that is shared by many black and Asian women. The history and the present state of the movement *does* make sense to a lot of us, but in an unassimilated, extraneous way. We have not participated in the processes that have led to the thinking of today. We did not identify the goals, or define our needs at all. And yet as women the movement proclaims to be ours, by definition.

Part of the problem has been that feminists have been too eager to teach and rescue, and not eager enough to learn from diversity, and all too often a Eurocentric view is thrown over all our lives, like clingfilm, to create a false homogeneity of values and perceptions.

These attitudes have made many black and Asian women feel that women's groups have been keen on increasing their numbers without enlarging their concepts to incorporate other visions and realities, and maybe even change

26

their own. They have failed to understand the dynamics that impel black and Asian women, and when they have acknowledged that conceptual differences do exist, the analysis and interpretations have been disappointingly simplistic.

So on to the tale proper and why it was that I cried for two weeks after my beautiful child Ari was born at the John Radcliffe Hospital in Oxford.

I cried, firstly because I had not wanted to want him so badly. It was 1978. In spite of my love and desire to have him, and 'optimum' childbirth conditions – as they say – nice house, caring husband, epidurals and Claire Rayner's lubricating advice on demand, the never-had-it-so-good feelings were constantly being overshadowed by a deep sense of sorrow. It felt like Ari had arrived into a no man's land, an orphanage. These feelings were so powerful they actually knocked against my ribs, for a fortnight. Now they just quietly tremble within, every time his security is threatened.

My mother, too, had wept when I had arrived into her life thirty years before. Our tears were not for the same reasons – she had cried because her life had stretched her out so painfully; she felt my birth was the final wrench on the rack that would make her snap into pieces. There she was in the hospital in Kampala, Uganda, with no money, a husband who had disappeared, two other children aged ten and eleven and a baby who was half dead, (my birth weight was three pounds) and half wanted at that.

They would not let her leave the hospital because she could not settle the bill. So a close family friend (male) rescued her. A whisper, which went on forever, swept through the town. This friend, they said, was obviously having an affair with my mother. It was because he was a *man* that his generosity was so unacceptable. The women in the community found this hard to forgive. He was infringing on their territory. They would never have let my mother

27

really sink. Being a mother had resulted in my mother becoming a 'whore' to the community. An indelibly hard experience and one that has never left her.

It made her ragingly strong too. Fiercely and bitterly independent of men, she has spent her entire life totally envious of other women in our community who were pampered by their husbands and spent their lives decking themselves and their homes, and as affluent middle-class women, doing little else.

She had to take control of her life in a way these women were never expected to. And it gave her no pride or satisfaction. Yet, she had proved herself so unique that secretly she became the local legend of the town. She had had the imagination to go out and train herself to teach, and she became the top primary school teacher in the town – much in demand for private tuition by the same people who had hurt her so much with their gossip and suspicion. This was the beginning of a commitment to education for girls in our society and my mother was, ironically, the role model for these incipient ambitions. Our lives were full of these contradictions – none of us believed that life was ever right angled. What was important was that my mother, Jena Damji, who at one time was shunned by some of her closest friends, in time, established an unshakeable position in the community once again.

My father's role in our lives remained peripheral throughout. He was an unusual man, bright but with no sense of responsibility or shame. He wanted to languish his life away in some kind of Victorian time warp, reading Dickens and lamenting the state of the world. It suited him just fine to have an independent wife. Especially one who was so very enterprising at managing finances – a word he particularly abhorred and with which he had nothing at all to do. Consequently, my mother's life for a few years was a nightmarish treadmill. After she had finished teaching, she catered for weddings and other occasions, and then way into the night sewed clothes for other people.

She was and is extraordinary, never flinching from life and maintaining a wry look at it all. I remember how amazed I was when I realised that, twice a week, she dressed up and went to the cinema entirely on her own. Not to the special 'Ladies' shows' for women like her, which were put on in the afternoon, but proper evening performances. And she refused all offers to go with other couples who offered to chaperone her. This was revolutionary then, and would be fairly revolutionary here and now.

Hers was a feminism thrust upon her. It was not a life she would have chosen, but it was one where she took power and began an important process of political analysis, of the position of men and women, using much of this in her teaching. I did not then make a connection with the word feminism, which I really only fell upon when I arrived here in the 1970s. At that time it just seemed another incomprehensible word in the huge wave that hit me, part of the great culture shock. And, in terms of important discoveries, came way below other exciting ones on the list, like instant food and tube trains.

It meant nothing more than that at the time, partly because of my own naïvety and also because of my irritation because all the froth seemed to be an indulgence that the West could afford with its belly full, and too much time and thought to spare. I had seen too much of the real struggles of life, to take seriously the ambling discourses on the oppression of women, by some of the most privileged women in the world, on the manicured lawns of Oxford.

I had seen my mother live through the agony of desperate shortages, manipulating loan sharks, take control of her life in a society where she had all the responsibilities and none of the privileges and rights given to the men. The other women in Africa had to face appalling problems for the same reasons. When I thought about that, these Oxford tea-party conversations, brilliant as they were in theory and thought, seemed flippant and irrelevant.

In many other ways too, my mother had seemed ahead of

her times in terms of how she brought us up. She was utterly determined that my sister and I should have a *better* education than my brother, because, she said, as a man he would make it anyway.

Never whining about her fate, or looking poor and defeated in any way, my mother had provided me with too strong an image of what the real battles for women were about, for me to be able to enthuse with the indolent women I met in Oxford, (what vast amounts of time were available to them to sit and *talk*) who rose to high-pitched passion over Kate Millett. There was also a coldness about these women, particularly when they discussed the 'tyranny' of childbirth and the child-rearing role. Of course their preoccupations were the same as mine, but it just seemed to be a different kind of struggle when the consequences in the lives of Asian and African women were so stark and unprotected.

There was a fundamental departure for me when we discussed children. Here we were worlds apart in our thinking. For my mother, having children and bringing them up had in effect meant a confirmation of her freedom – she had proved that it could be done without a man – proof that women were strong and indestructible. There was never a sense of conflict, or a feeling of being drained of her selfhood, or of being flooded over by the experience of motherhood. It was a vital addition, an extension of her strength. It gave her a boost, an electric current which even now, in her seventies, she looks back at with satisfaction and pride. The way her three children have turned out is tangible proof of her resilience and creativity. Particularly the fact that she did it on her own. The internal imagery of childbearing and child-rearing in this country seems to me quite different from what it symbolises for me. The strong sense of the child being a burden you unload at some stage of your life, or the process of childbirth and nurturing as something that draws from a woman her selfhood making her socially and politically powerless, are alien images to me. When I was growing up, having a child gave a woman more power than anything else she could do. Physically, it was a growth, an addition to what she was, emotionally, it made her more substantial, complete and mature. The child was not a temporary resident in your life, but deeply and permanently knotted in with your being. There is no letting go of that bond the way there is in this society; when our children grow up here and assert the need to break that bond, it causes acute pain and sorrow, particularly to the women.

In my experience the strong bonds extended beyond the immediate family to the community itself. When my mother was struggling to bring us up, she was never really alone. *Nobody* was, in the symbiotic community we lived in in East Africa. The Asians living there had evolved a very strong network, partly because of the needs and fears that inevitably arise when groups emigrate, and partly because they were a minority in countries where they had no political power and a constant sense of being vulnerable. So you always knew that when the crunch came, the community would gather their resources and you would not drown – even when they disapproved. We had no children's homes, orphanages, etc. As a community we never needed them.

So, although people in the community found my mother's clearheaded independence and refusal to cower occasionally irritating, they would never have allowed her to go under. We did not live in an individualistic culture. Each life was connected to the collective well-being of the group, which functioned well because it was such an inter-related galaxy. When a child was born, in the truest sense, therefore, it belonged to us all. How I bring up my child is the concern of all those around me. It would never occur to me to say to these people that what I did with my child was my business or that he 'belonged' to me. They intervene all the time and my child is well protected by their involvement in his life.

31

Individual motherhood is not diminished by this collective responsibility. Some of the most moving poetry and popular music in our lives is a celebration of the mother/child relationship. The first song my mother ever sang to me is one of these and it rises in my head whenever she is away and I miss her. It speaks of how she would 'Tuck me away in her heart' when the thunderstorms came and the world got too noisy for me. 'Only your mother has that hiding place in her heart', the song says.

It is a recognition of the unique nurturing that only a mother can give a child. This often leads to very intense mother/child relationships. Even grown up, children find an extraordinary overt display of love from their mothers. When I visit my mother, she does not sleep until I am well tucked up in bed, or eat until I have eaten. The relationship is very tactile too and a mother is seen as the communicator of the central social values that hold the community together.

But around that relationship, there are several protective circles to catch you if you fall and catch the child if you let go. It is a liberating concept, though it can also be coercive. And it is something I desperately miss since my dislocated life here started, especially since my son was born. There was real freedom for a mother in those endless circles. You knew there were others who could protect your child, sometimes even from the emotional excesses you produced. You did not suffer from the agonising, immobilising fear that is produced by extreme feelings of possession. Although the mother/child bond was deep, it did not revolve around the feelings of ownership, which tend to debilitate any relationship. If you own something, particularly something precious, you live in fear that you will lose it, someone will covet it and the terrible weight of responsibility towards it can be crushing.

This can happen easily in nuclear family structures where the feelings of child ownership are strong. This inevitably leads to the mothers becoming the sole satisfactory providers of children's emotional needs. This attitude permeates right through this society, from those right-wingers who want to get mothers back to the kitchen sink, so their children will be better brought up and not turn to crime, to the half-apologetic new woman who guiltily tells you about her wonderful new nanny. It is a stranglehold that will take centuries to eradicate.

It has always seemed to me that that kind of exclusive ownership and dependency must create intolerable internal tensions, especially when there are so many other social changes and moving targets to cope with at the same time. So, a woman has the right to have all the life experiences, positions, etc. that a man has, but when she has a child, the relationship she has with her child is considered so all-embracing that she has no room for guilt-free emotional movement or accommodation of her needs. In our community, within the fold, a child was woven into a multiplicity of relationships, each one well defined and distinct, but quite capable of sustaining a child. A cousin was brought up by his uncle and aunt because they were childless. They lived round the corner from his real parents and siblings. No one pretended that he lived with his real parents. He had four parents, two names for mother, two for father.

There was never a sense of competitiveness between parents that you find here. Particularly in these times of the new father encroaching on that inside territory that used to be ours as women and ours alone. Questions that need to be asked have simply not been asked about these new developments. When fathers get as involved as they do in the childbirth and child-rearing roles, are they competing for space they feel they have been denied before, or is it a genuine cooperative impulse that will liberate women from some of the oppression they felt before? Can men be trusted that much?

When my mother worked, I had an entire corridor of women from the flats next door, who were my surrogate mothers. The men barely existed for the children except as financial providers, and the occasional settling of minor

domestic disturbances. Otherwise they were pretty super-
fluous. If the women complained, it was usually a series of
well-rehearsed moans which felt like a chorus of bad jokes
and little else. The only serious problem for the women was
financial unreliability – and sometimes male violence. This,
when discovered – and it was not possible to hide it in the
kind of lives we led – was dealt with efficiently by community leaders .

The women did not expect emotional support, nurturing
love, and excitement from the men. Their most enjoyable
social occasions were with other women, and most of what
they did was within that female world. They were less
likely, therefore, to be disappointed by the kind of usual
experiences of male indifference. In that sense they were
profoundly liberated in the way those of us brought up on
romantic mythologies never are. It was because some of
these codes were broken by my mother that she had
problems getting support in the early days after my birth.
And in a strange way she has never understood the strength
of this network and what it gave her.

In our case, as even the financial role had been relinquished by my erratic and undependable father, new
ground had to be broken by my mother. He was not an
uncaring man, simply a bohemian who ought not to have
had a family. He never made a single decision in the family.
He was relieved at being relieved of such distractions. For
him, it was extremely important for my mother to assume
total independence and for us to do the same. It was an
entirely selfish and self-serving strategy. He was free of guilt
and his basic function of hunter-gatherer.

In important ways therefore I had already found in my
mother what my white friends in Oxford were earnestly
mulling over. I had grown up in the midst of a powerful
practical display of the independence and power of women.
It is in the nature of such things, where so many generalisations abound about the lives of Asian women, that most
expectations are confounded. Received wisdom often has it

that these women live in a state of total subjugation, and like most generalisations, there is much that is true in this perception. But, underneath the rigidity and conformism, some freedoms were and are seized by women like my mother. It is a skill and strategy younger Asian women like myself are rapidly losing as we settle down in the West.

That particular sisterhood had an organic closeness that is not really easily found here. There is much talk of women here 'networking' but it just does not feel the same. Perhaps this is taking a dangerously idealistic view of adversity, but real pressures do seem to create real resistence movements and an undercover life full of espionage.

The context is also important. The dominant philosophy in the West is divisive, splitting people into egocentric little atoms, people so split think primarily of themselves, and they are at a loss to know how to give up a little of that self and form genuine rooted human links.

Feminism, which needs to have a collective agenda, is battling away at a structural beam of this society. And there are many fears around the demands of this kind of thinking. People are afraid that if they extend and give themselves, the 'me' in them will be diminished, or lose shape. This leads to a more selfish concept of corporate life, under which lies the deepest fear of all – that there is a finite store of emotional substance in a person and that the principles of good housekeeping need to apply to how you use it.

This concept remains totally alien to me. Our inner world tells us that the more you give, the more you grow. There is no panic about the gradual erosion of the self through the giving of yourself to others. That is why having a child is seen as an extension of the self and not a reduction of it. A belief of this sort has valuable practical implications. A large number of Asian women in this country work. Their children are well cared for within the fold of the family, where the women who do the caring feel neither resentful nor noble for being there when needed.

But it is difficult to keep this up after the kinds of

upheavals that the Ugandian Asian community has been through. In many ways the centre was shattered in 1972 when Idi Amin ordered them out of Uganda. They were scattered, carrying seeds of their past lives in their pockets, unsure whether they would ever find suitable soil to plant them. Mostly they didn't. And we are still in that flux.

This background is essential to understand the feelings of loss and fear I experienced when my son was born. Especially in terms of what Britain had begun to mean to me then. That had been another psychological earthquake. In the hospital they called it post-natal depression. I think it was a watershed time when my past identity, personal and political, had crashed into the new bits and pieces that had begun to grow since I had arrived here, including all the contradictions I have been describing.

I had lived in Britain at the time for six years, having left Uganda, only slightly reluctantly, to come to what had then seemed to be the centre of the universe. For the six years strange experiences and stranger philosophies had rained down on my head like endless coloured balls, confusing, irritating, scary, and exhilarating. I had also learnt the art of navel gazing, (or self-analysis) and self-absorption, which was extremely pleasurable at first, naughty but nice, and thoroughly improper in terms of how I had been brought up, where other people always came first.

Motherhood only helped to underscore all of these and other shaking upheavals in my life at the time. For twenty-three years I had lived in Uganda, the youngest daughter in an odd family where all the rigid norms of Asian society were tilted, but which never led to any rejections from that society.

But here the country I had arrived in, the 'motherland' had shown appalling signs of neglect and irresponsibility towards us, her 'coloured' children from the colonies who had so eagerly come seeking warm embracing arms. Britain had proved the political harlot, slipping her eyes away as we approached, muttering under her breath that we didn't really belong to her. Later on, she was to get more brazen, suggesting that we were threatening imposters and then justifying her betrayal by passing laws to keep us at bay.

At the beginning, I had chosen to ignore this betrayal and found excuses in my heart that these were merely fond chidings from an over-strict parent and that in some ways Britain did not really mean it. So in the early days, I was to be found swishing around Oxford in Laura Ashley gowns going for cream teas in pretty little lairs in the area. Attempts at assimilation of the least profound kind. I was also taken up with my life with my beautiful husband (also from Uganda) and idyllic marriage. Unlike my mother's generation, by the time we left Uganda, the younger girls had begun their romance with 'love' and I had begun to think that here lay the way to all happiness. So it was easy getting entwined into the curiously restraining notion — love.

What I sought then, and found, was a life totally unlike the one my mother had lived through. I wanted to be nourished, cherished and spoilt by a man. The Doll's House wife. My husband was everything my father had never been. He was soft, passionate, conventional and unspeakably responsible. What was more, he was fast shedding those unfashionable tendencies of chauvinism he had with him when he had first arrived from Uganda, proving himself to be a delightful egalitarian partner.

Two parallel romances were thus being conducted at the same time. The first with the country of my dreams and the other with my marriage. Perhaps another reason why meeting feminist women in Oxford was so disconcerting was that it didn't tally with the tough life I had known before and it also interfered with the dreams I had since conjured up for my own life. So strong women terrified me, and talk about female equality irritated me. I also felt completely alone, away from those women I had been with in my childhood, who with their wisdom and love had softened so many blows and sheltered me.

For the first time in my life, I was entirely dependent on a man for all my emotional sustenance. Romantically, this was thrilling, but inside, I felt alone and afraid, as my sense of identity rattled about making hollow noises. It was all this that had made me wait a long time before I had a child, in spite of the fact that both of us had wanted one. The night Ari was born all these feelings, conflicts and uncertainties surfaced in an acute way.

It felt so strange in the hospital that night. My husband, well oiled by then in the ways of modern childbirth, had done all the right things, and was anxiously awaiting the results while playing scrabble which the forward looking hospital had provided for him. I had to have my mother there too, because it just did not feel right without her. The two did not mix well at all. Unease rapidly set in. None of us knew what to do. My husband was, officially, on female territory. I did not know if I wanted to be a modern young miss or creep back into the folds of what I knew and loved best. My mother, whose suspicions about men were still red-ripe, saw his presence as an infringement of our basic rights as women. I found myself playing a part for the first time against my real instincts, falling in too willingly with the expected norms of this society. Meanwhile, my mother waited outside for seven hours, with no role to play. It was a painful birth, and the pain added to the general feeling that I was somehow not performing in the right way washed up between so many different expectations.

There were other fears too. When Ari emerged from my body, I was so afraid that I was ejecting him into a world that would reject him because he was not a white. I felt guilty for doing this to him, and a heavy sense of responsibility of having to protect him from it all. I felt possessive too, and this was a new feeling. Ari was obviously a symbol of a lot of things; the bond between my husband and myself, someone I had deeply loved, and love still, despite the fact that ten years on from that moment he walked away from me and the seething life of a pre-pubescent son.

Ari represented a final settling down in this country, the next generation of the unwanted.

And as he grew older and proved himself the exceptional child, my husband continued to play the role of equal carer and sharer. The entire culture of my family began to change as a result of this. All of a sudden, my mother's scepticism about my husband turned to spellbound adoration. Every time he changed a nappy, not only were all cultural expectations altered, but my mother's views started to shift in subtle ways. She moved in to look after Ari six weeks after I had had him. I felt no jealousy at all. She was much better than I was at providing basic primary care for him. I felt free to love and spoil and know him. He could not have had a better mother than my mother, and in a fundamental way that is what she will always be to him. Her attitude towards me was odd though. She was often angry with me for asserting my independence in my relationship, which I was beginning to do. She wanted me to join in the worship of my husband with her. It was all a desperately confusing time for me.

There were many other collisions going on in my head at the same time. I could not work out how I was going to stop myself overprotecting my son from the dangers of being born Asian in a racist country. I could not decide if his dependence on me gave me power or assigned me to a low status position in life. I yearned for the certainties of the past and yet knew that I could not have survived the experiences my mother went through when she had me.

The fact that Ari is a boy and a very masculine boy, made the dynamics even more interesting. My mother and I obviously feed his inexhaustible ego. He is often aloof and does manipulate the sentimentality of his mother and grandmother. When his father was around there was less of this, but there were other things that were equally alarming. Ari saw through the façade of equality, and picked up all the unexpected sexist attitudes. His more active interests were directed at his dad and he constantly turned to me for emotional massaging. These were stereotypes I did not enjoy, but there was little I could do about it. When he fell and hurt himself his father asked him why he had not been more careful while I wiped his tears.

He does see great strengths, both in my mother and in myself and is always delighted to tell his friends that I do an 'important' job, and that I can tell off waiters in no uncertain terms. He is also deeply ashamed of these goings-on in public. For Ari and me the hardest lessons are only just being learnt. Ten days before his tenth birthday, the perfect father and husband walked out of our lives with his young blonde mistress, rocking us all with a sense of betrayal and shock. And as the debris still falls down from the ceiling, my son asks all the time why he did it, would I ever do it, and do men do this more often than women? Having been nourished on all kinds of sweet expectations of marital love, I too feel hostage to those bewildering feelings. And it is only the wisdom of my mother, back to her original position on men, with a vengeance, that keeps us going.

Ari was six when he started teasing me about a fantasy he had. He said he wanted the three of us to live in a cottage where I would be called Annabel, wear checked pinafores and bake bread and cakes all day long. He and his dad would go out on adventures and come home in the evening and tell me all about their adventures while I served them food.

Last week, he hugged me and said; 'Don't cry mum, you are not Annabel, remember.'

Katherine Gieve

And Not To Count the Cost

The house is empty. I walk around it and nothing has moved since I last looked. No chaos has mushroomed into the ordered rooms. Sterile? Certainly unaccustomed. The children have gone to stay with their grandparents. I cannot use the time fruitfully but sit and dream.

Daniel is seven, Matthew, five, and when I think about the past seven years I feel like a person watching the dust begin to settle after an earthquake. Seismic tremors still shoot through my life, but not perhaps so frequently nor quite so catastrophically as they did in earlier years. I am promised a period of relative calm until the shock waves of

41

adolescence begin. I can see now that I have moved to something more ordinary, away from that curious state of grace: of charged experience and feeling – both pleasure and pain – of living with children in their very early years.

I had my first child when I was thirty, after dormant teenage years followed by exciting twenties when I gradually came out of hibernation and realised that I might be an actor in the world – not just a spectator. The women's movement was the mainspring of my adult life, which gave me a political perspective of the things that needed to be done and also the confidence and support to play a part in trying to do some of them. It also gave me a personal perspective which helped me to understand my earlier inaction. But the 'me' I had discovered or created during those years still seemed a fragile thing – my earlier dreamy, drifting nature not far away – and so while I wished for a baby, I was afraid. Women's liberation had provided an escape route from the enforced femininity and passivity required of girls in the suburb where I grew up. I was afraid that I might be submerged again and that my identity and purpose as an adult would be lost.

What would motherhood mean? In some sense giving up yourself, putting the needs of others first; answering demands and not making them. There is associated with the idea of motherhood a singular universal imperative of generosity and self-sacrifice which threatens to extinguish individuality. For me, it echoed that earlier time when I seemed to lack a self and a direction.

I did desire a baby. It was not so much a wish for children, for a family, but a powerful physical longing. I became pregnant but waited for the baby anxiously, thinking that I should resist and not be swept away by motherhood. The reality was both more overwhelming and entrancing than I could have dreamed. The demands of the baby seemed infinite, and he the most perfect and beautiful of all babies. Days ran into nights of constant feeding, changing, holding, carrying, comforting. Immediately after his birth I could not think of satisfying his needs, and with relief watched his father and grandmother as they looked after him. I only wanted him to be asleep, moving gently as he had done inside me. We had talked a lot about looking after the baby together: how important it was for John to learn to comfort him and change him so that he did not relate vicariously through me. But the idea of my sharing the care of the baby was a curious one when I seemed to have lost the baby. I had a sense of doubled loss; I missed the baby, no longer inside me and I had lost John's love for the baby in me. I was delighted with John's uninhibited love and competence, but even then I felt confused: who am I in all this? My initial relief at not being required to be maternal, since I did not feel maternal, was mixed with a feeling that I should have a special place. I remember with peculiar joy my first day all alone with Daniel some three weeks later.

Time passed, my parents went home and John went back to work. I, during my maternity leave, was alone responsible for the baby during the days. The struggle which ensued was not, as I had anticipated, between the baby's needs and my need for my own autonomy and independent identity – but the more complex struggle between my desire for autonomy and my desire and pleasure in satisfying the baby. My two selves, as it seemed, struggled against each other. In retrospect I think the argument went on in my head; in practice the demands of the baby imposed a greater imperative. When I was with him, I responded to his demands and his rhythms. I was astonished at what seemed like the total invasion of the baby into every minute of my day and night and at my own willingness and capacity to answer his needs. Someone asked me a few weeks after his birth whether I managed to get out at all. I remember answering that I was not much interested in getting out. In the months that followed I tried to complete my own projects in the margins of the day, still thinking that if I did not do so I would be lost.

*

'Motherhood is the most basic of all the relationships. It starts off with complete clarity on the part of the baby who does all the talking.' *Amanda Faulkner, artist*

One of the most surprising things about my relationship with Daniel was the way in which he seemed to create me. My wish not to succumb to him was set at nothing by his own certainty. Whilst I did not acknowledge myself as the only principal in his life, I did acquiesce to him. Indeed, my life seemed plastic in the face of his demands: a minute by minute see-saw of feeling: moments of bliss and physical joy followed by perfect peace, then sometimes in seconds I was thrown into desperation. My diary, six weeks after his birth, records a turmoil not unusual in those early days:

> J. and his mother gone around 9.00 a.m. D. very sleepy – but not asleep. Grouchy. Didn't want to eat anymore, so we walked around the house. Didn't want to play – didn't get it together to sleep. Finally went to sleep in my arms and I transferred him to basket after several tries around 9.30 a.m. So I had breakfast and looked at the headlines – washed up and cleared up a bit. D. still asleep so I made some phone calls and he woke and wouldn't settle. Should I make a rush to leave the house while he's awake in the hope he would sleep in the pram or try to settle him first so there was time to collect things to go out. He looked hungry, fed him – he goes half asleep but wakes on the way to the basket – decide to change him in anticipation of his usual big sleep. Change him, cuddle him, he goes to sleep in the basket. Take advantage of silence to put nappies in wash. He screams half way but is comforted. Up again to finish nappies. This is wonderful, asleep at last. Maybe I shouldn't go out at all. Much easier to work at home.

It seems extraordinary now how closely linked I was with every second of his life and how great was my need for him to be asleep so that I could have a little space of my own. With Matthew I could co-exist with his waking times. I did not need him to be asleep in the same way.

I came to see how much I had relinquished my autonomy when later, Daniel, then aged between two and three, began most emphatically to separate himself from me. I was by then used to being on the same side as him in a democratic and symbiotic way. He had created, I felt, a responsive, acquiescent mother, only then to turn me into something quite different. There began a series of fights of the let-me-do-it-myself kind, and a series of demands – not intended to be met – like revolutionary demands designed to expose the limits of tolerance. 'I want the white cup, no, the blue cup, not that one, the one with the red handle.' Demands designed to sort out whether I was his right hand and ultimately to assert his own independence. His inquiries seemed directed no longer to the external world. He appeared to be exploring my internal world which we both discovered contained unknown recesses of exasperation and anger. Democracy did not work; until I found, painfully, that the descent of equals into a chaos of misery was disastrous, I did not stand firm. Eventually, I was created into another sort of mother, again it seemed by his imperative. This time not 'maternal acquiescent' but 'maternal firm and autocratic'.

Neither role could I have imagined – nor would I have chosen. The challenge to my autonomy which these transformations wreaked was unexpected. It was not the hard work of childcare that I found so difficult (probably because I shared it with others) but the constantly changing relationship which continued in terms not chosen by me at an unpredictable and changeable pace. It required constant reassessment and with it pain, anger and remorse, as well as excitement and pleasure. Daniel elicited from me both my greatest love and generosity and my darkest anger and frustration.

*

If I did not resist the baby, I did, for a long time, resist the idea of being a mother; I saw myself, initially, as a special companion. I think this was partly because of my fear for my identity, partly because I wanted to leave space for John and for Sue Sawyer (who looked after Daniel when I went back to work) to establish their own relationships with him. There was the notion of exclusive possession in motherhood that I wanted to avoid. Just as I wanted to avoid matching myself against the archetypes of self-sacrifice – mother, teacher, provider. Yet, the relationship was not just one between two individuals, despite my wish to define it only in that way. Inevitably, I had expectations of what mothers ought to be and it was difficult to escape from them. What is confusing about the ideals of motherhood is their apparent simplicity and stability. There is nothing to prepare one for the fact that to be a mother is to have a complex relationship with another individual from which one cannot escape. It was for me a relationship that seemed to be subject to external direction, created in part by the baby whom I felt set his own agenda, and in part by the irresistible force in me to try to respond to his demands, in order to create harmony and calm, and to satisfy him. It was this particular need to 'make things all right' and the impossibility of doing so that finally drew me into accepting my role as a mother and into appreciating the epic nature of my experience.

To be kissed better is the child's expectation of the mother and to kiss better is the mother's hope of herself; to take away the pain and bring peace in its place is to be a good mother. Why do all those baby care manuals not tell us how difficult it is? We cannot kiss better all the suffering even in our own homes. Some problems may be managerial: better planning, fewer tears, less exhaustion, less sorrow. But when my first child says to me as I feed the second child; 'Go away – don't let me see you feed him', this is a sorrow too profound to kiss better. I go into another room to feed the baby; the first runs in, 'Mummy, come, the sitting room is on fire.' Management may help, but it is not the answer to jealousy. Books don't tell of the darkness of passions and how to live with them or how to cope with anger and remorse. Glimpses and echoes can be found in fairy stories and poems. One of Matthew's favourite rhymes for a time reveals a terrible level of ferocity. Did he like to bring to the surface all our violent feelings?

GIANT BONAPARTE

Baby, baby, naughty baby,
Hush you squalling thing I say,
Peace, this moment, peace or may be
Bonaparte will come this way.

Baby, baby he's a giant,
Tall and black as Rouen steeple,
And he breakfasts, dines, rely on't,
Every day on naughty people.

Baby, baby, if he hears you,
As he gallops past the house,
Limb from limb at once he'll tear you,
Just as pussy tears a mouse.

And he'll beat you, beat you, beat you,
And he'll beat you all to pap,
And he'll eat you, eat you, eat you,
Every morsel, snap, snap, snap.

Despite an intellectual recognition that all needs cannot be satisfied I still felt that it should be possible. On bad days, sometimes bad weeks in winter, my failure to cope turned to anger and frustration and, then, many times a day I tried to start at the beginning – with optimism and generosity, as I reminded myself how much larger I was than the children. Coming to terms with the lack of reciprocity, when I had come to expect reciprocity in all my other relationships, was a difficult task. It took me back to a prayer said many times at school:

> To give and not to count the cost
> To fight and not to heed the wounds
> To toil and not to seek for rest
> To labour and not to ask for any reward
> Save that of knowing that we do thy will.

It was hard to live without reciprocity but harder still to realise that to make things all right was often not within my gift. There was a level at which I could not assuage the pain of the jealous child, nor lessen my own grief at finding him so difficult to love. To make amends we went on outings, just him and me. 'Did you have a good time,' asked Sue. 'It was cold, bitterly cold,' he said. It seemed it took a lifetime to realise that the drama played out in our kitchen was a Greek tragedy: that hatred could run side by side with love and that love could be renewed and could heal some of the hurt. I could not escape my own central place in this story.

Times of particular desperation usually took place when I was alone with the children, and in general my experience made me think critically again about the nuclear family. Simone de Beauvoir (who did not have children) writes in *The Second Sex*, 'it would be desirable for the child to be left to his parents infinitely less than at present, and for his studies and diversions to be carried on among other children, under the direction of adults whose bonds with him would be impersonal and pure.' This struck a chord with me. Could it be good for the children to live in such an emotional atmosphere? And yet I do not think de Beauvoir has the answer. She imagines that non-parents can escape the intensity of the adult/child relationship. This may be true in part, but children are not given to maintaining bonds that are impersonal and pure – whether they are with their parents or with others they elicit a commitment and they make continuous demands. A tolerance for extreme feelings is part of the experience. The problems of passivity, the need for acquiescence in looking after small children is not only a problem for their parents but also for others looking after them. The need to listen and to respond must be present if bringing up children is not to be frustrating for everyone. If, as an adult, you try hard to follow your own scheme of things, the child becomes nothing but an irritant. And for a child to have such a companion must provoke a crippling sense of powerlessness.

I returned to work, after my maternity leave for each child, to maintain an income and my (future) career. I worked part time and it provided a great relief from the exhaustion of life at home. I was struck by the enormous contrast between work at the office and work at home. It was as though life took place on different planets. Life at home is a life of subsistence and survival with the constant repetition of daily tasks: to feed and clothe, and to clothe and feed and comfort. I felt a sense of women as the repository of timelessness and of continuity without progress. There are parallels, but the world of outside work is distinct in so many significant ways from childcare. At home there are no measurable rewards, financial or otherwise, nor is there a similar sense of achievement, though there is certainly satisfaction. The means/ends character of the market place, with tasks completed ticked off on a list, projects brought to fruition, has little place in caring for children. It is true that domestic tasks do have that quality and for that reason the drudgery can sometimes be an oddly restoring accompaniment to childcare. At least there is a beginning, a middle and an end to the cycle of washing – if you are allowed to get to the end.

As to the achievements in the children, the achievements are theirs. They learn to crawl, to walk, to speak, with exemplary application – with vigorous unalienated labour. Certainly, they need you, they need companionship, but you cannot look at your children and see the effects of your efforts in a direct and detailed way. There are none of the conventional satisfactions of a job well done. Not only is a child not a product of your labour in any ordinary sense, but I think it is also very important for the child that he or she should not be.

Yet, despite the drama of home life in contrast with even the most fraught days at the office, I was drawn to be at home. I didn't feel particularly that the children needed me nor did I feel a moment's doubt about their other caretaker, Sue – but I still wanted to be with them in all the morass and confusion, as well as for the peaceful times – delicious summer days in the park and successful afternoons with friends. But to mix work and home was difficult. Being with the children could not easily be squashed into limited periods of time; a whole day would give enough time for highs and lows, time for the resolution of combat, small breaks when both children might sleep or, at least, rest. Whereas if I worked for a half a day I would be faced, usually, with only the waking times; and when I did a full day and returned from work in the evening the crescendo of emotion was often too much to cope with, pitched as I still was at a brisk productive work pace, unable to slow down and listen to the children. I found that the more time I spent with the children, the easier and more enjoyable it was.

Part-time work has been a solution of sorts for which I am grateful. It has given me the opportunity to keep doing work I enjoy and find interesting although I have often felt an inadequate colleague. It has also allowed me to spend time at home and with other women who have children to look after. My need for their support and companionship has been great – to while away the time as the children pottered together; to discuss again and again the vagaries of their development. In these conversations – denigrated as women's talk, baby talk – we tried to get to grips with the complexities of power relations; to face the disconcerting way in which the sequence of a child's development may refuse to follow his or her chronological age; my wonderful Matthew, strong and independent, is suddenly a baby again. His beautiful sentences degenerate into a language, it would seem, constructed to set my teeth on edge; and it is impossible for him to put his socks on. First, I find myself impatient, resistant and unloving. He regresses further. I pause, breathe deeply and try to find the courage and tolerance to love him as he wants to be loved, and help him in the next stage of his heroic struggle to grow up. I turn to my friends to ask, 'Does it help him if I pander to him, who is meant to be the boss?'

For all this we need time for ourselves and love from others. We need companionship from people who find our children lovable when we ourselves find them impossible to love, and who will delight in them as we do: people who are willing to acknowledge the difficulty of the task.

Four days before Daniel was born I wrote in my diary:

What will life be like? Will I look at things with the same eyes again? Remember, it is the baby's beginning – neither the beginning nor the end of me. I hope. Sitting suspended on the edge of time. No idea of the character or feelings of the future. Who will the baby be?

I did not imagine the force or the excitement – nor how I would willingly be taken over by my children. But I feel extended, and not diminished, by life without aims and objectives, as well as by the intensity and physical pleasure of being with them. I look at the world with different eyes and inward with a new vision. I feel riven, torn apart and made again.

Victoria Hardie

The World Became
a More Dangerous Place

My first son George was born dead, revived and put in an incubator. I came round from the anaesthetic to see an empty cot at the end of my bed. The paediatrician told me in a matter-of-fact way, that if he survived the first twenty-four hours without fits, which could either brain damage or kill him, then he would live to be a healthy boy.

George is now ten years old, has a younger brother called Harry, likes making garlic bread and wants to fly the Concorde.

The despair I sunk into during those first twenty-four hours of my son's life made me feel as if I was going mad. I am not a Christian, but I made a pact with God. I would never be unkind or jealous; I would never lie, cheat, gloat, or snarl when doing housework. Anyone could have done what they wanted to me as long as George survived. Childcare books I had read hadn't dealt with the trauma of a birth gone wrong.

52

Notions of independence and continuing with my writing so carefully worked out before the birth seemed an unnecessary luxury as George progressed in his incubator.

Our small farmhouse in North Herefordshire into which I had put the last of my money awaited us. My husband and I envisaged a romantic country upbringing, filled with pets, fresh vegetables and peace for us to write in. I believed I was doing the 'right thing' in raising children away from the city, its filth and lack of space.

I was to discover as time went on that it wasn't just emotional vulnerability that hit me, but physical and economic vulnerability as well. The world suddenly became a much more dangerous place once I had a baby dependent on me for his very life. For the first time I was thrown into a world that did not recognise my physical, emotional, social and political needs. This applied to design, architecture, roads, public transport, dangerous machinery; not to mention lack of community childcare facilities. Emotionally, the need for self-expression, the safety valve of economic independence, as well as the intense need for a close bond with my son was a subject not confronted by classes, clinics or institutions that rule family lives. By the time George reached school age it was clear to me that society is run on the basis that all working folk are childless, or if they are not, that they have an underpaid or unpaid domestic worker to enable them to work as if they were childless. Mothers are employed in spite of being mothers, not because they are mothers. The perceptions and experiences gained through motherhood are rarely used in the 'official' marketplace unless they fit in with the traditional institution or work structure. My observations made me feel threatened. The feeling I kept getting was that mothers don't count. Whoever invented the phrase, 'Women and children first', spoke to deaf ears. By the time I had my second son Harry, these resentments didn't hit me so hard because I was better prepared. It isn't the child that makes your life hard, it is the response of the adult world and the powers that be. It is, usually, the very people who sentimentalise and idealise motherhood who stop listening.

The conflicting pictures I had of motherhood as I grew up had never been an inspiration and they contributed to my postponing creating a family until I was thirty years old. Then a manic broodiness took over and I'm glad it did. But the listless and trapped mothers I knew of bore no relation to the idealistic images in children's books, films, and ads. Images that depicted children who always went to bed at the drop of a train set, just as 'Daddy', (James Stewart or John Wayne), came home from the office, or after rounding up a few cows, with a proud beam at spotless kiddies, ready to read them a bedtime story; whilst mother looked serenely on in an ironed frock, a candlelit dinner at the ready, with sparkling eyes brimming with fulfilment – and certainly no dark circles under them.

These images contrasted with the reality: Daddy exploding with irritation at a Mercedes Benz on the hall floor, or a T-shirt flung on the back of a sofa, or finger marks on the telly screen. An explosion brought on by a hard day at the office and an expectation of what family life and the perfect mother ought to be like. Perhaps Mummy hadn't, for example, been able to buy a great dinner because she'd been waiting in all day for a plumber who never arrived. Although she may have tidied up the toys over and over, when her back was turned, they had been tipped on the floor again.

On celluloid there was an ironed check tablecloth and a fire roaring – potent images of security and love. They were images that appealed to me, because, above all, I wanted my children to be secure. This idealistic view conflicted with memories of my mother. One of the most anxious memories I have of her was the discovery of a bank statement on her desk which read, 'Overdrawn £50'. In the 1950s this was a great deal of money and I was plagued with worry for her. How was she going to ask my father for money without there being a row? Another time, I remember her laughing because I thought she hadn't any money to travel home after she had seen me off on the train to boarding school. I was aware at a very early age that my mother was vulnerable because she depended on my father's approval for our survival, not to mention other unknown faces, named but not yet understood; offices, train services, banks, bosses, lawyers, which I now know to be various institutions, political and otherwise, that rule all our lives. The vulnerability she gave off was also present in my aunts.

The mothers nearer my generation seemed to be trapped somewhere in the middle. They tended to be juggling full-time or part-time jobs plus family, clearly finding the situation emotionally and physically shattering. In some cases their pay only just covered their child-minding expenses. They vibrated unspoken anxieties and insecurities, as if life would collapse at the sign of a temperature or a disappearing nanny. The nanny sometimes disappeared with the husband thus taking practical, financial and moral support away, to boot.

Mothers seemed to be ridiculed, feared or fawned over. The wife and mother, always someone to escape from, had nowhere to escape to. She would always be there, ready with a hot meal, a welcome or a chastisement. Husbands became offspring to their wives. Mothers who chose to work or had to go out to work were considered basically uncaring.

I wanted to be different. I wanted to work and yet be very involved with George. Also, I arrogantly believed that I would raise my children 'better' than my mother and I would not be stuck as a housewife, living through my husband's knowledge of the world outside the home. But the minute I was a mother things didn't turn out that way quite so easily.

When we first moved to Herefordshire the women in the local village three miles away were friendly but guarded.

This was partly due to me being from London and them being wary of 'townies' putting up house prices for weekend retreats, thus denying local people affordable houses in their own and only community. Once we established that our house was our only home the local mood towards us was warmer. But it was not possible for me to conform to the rural customs expected of rural women, particularly wives. It came as a shock to be asked by way of polite conversation on which day of the week I hung my washing out. Or on which day my husband let me go to the pub with him. It only bothered me because it bothered them that I didn't have a set domestic routine that they could identify with.

The village shop was on the corner of the market square which looked like a tourist's view of rural England. Black-and-white Tudor houses and cottages perched wonkily around the horse troughs in the centre. Elizabethan Coca Cola cans and beer crates stacked outside the half-timbered pub where once the picturesque drunken customers had weaved their way onto the A44 into the night. Tired farmers, salesmen on the road, visiting colour supplement journalists, a widow or two, cheque-book gypsies in search of a 1960s caravan trail or an Alfred Watkins ley line.

The woman who ran the village shop informed me that she knew I was pregnant – the farmer's wife had told her. Soon the other women in the village knew, and although I had kept the information to myself, my husband had mentioned it, and news in sparsely populated rural areas travels fast. An invite from the Women's Institute was promptly issued. It was as if they were saying, 'Now you'll know what life is really like.' Thrilled to be pregnant as I was, their attitude and the feeling that I was being brought down a peg or two confused me. I didn't need to be brought down, as I was then an unperformed playwright. And a silence pervaded as to what 'life' really would be like as a mother.

As my pregnancy progressed I became obsessed with the

way the house worked. Before conception I detested house-work and still do. Unless it was in proportion to writing, spending time with friends, pottering about, reading, and other more pleasurable activities. As I expanded I washed clothes, floors and just about everything else, over and over.

Mastermind, the rat that refused to die and lived in the barn adjoining the house gave me sleepless nights. I would wake my husband in the night and go on about tales of rats gnawing through walls and eating babies in their cots and various morbid reflections to which mothercare booklets didn't have answers. The relief was intense when a tinker friend left his Jack Russell dog in the barn for a night and ended Mastermind's concrete dinners, and my nightmares.

Just in time for George's birth I planted a vegetable garden and wrote a play. George's room was painted and as it was above the kitchen it was heated by the Rayburn stove underneath. The cot remained stacked in the corner until we were both safely back from hospital. A touch of supersti-tion there.

On my return, with George, to our farmhouse directly after the birth, the farmer's wife from over the road cooked me a meal. I was touched as her whole life seemed to be one of self-sacrifice anyway. She was her husband's telephone answerer, VAT form filler in, cook, babysitter, and what's more he wouldn't let her drive his new Volvo. She would only go to WI meetings if they didn't coincide with his bridge nights. A not untypical life-style for a farmer's wife.

It was a strain lifted to have the odd meal cooked for me in the time immediately following the birth because I needed all the rest I could get between feeds. I needed proper nourishing meals – I was breastfeeding which made me very hungry. When I look at myself in photographs taken soon after George was born, I seem to radiate happiness and fulfilment, and weigh about half a stone more than I did before conception. Maybe this euphoria was because George was the first of two planned and much wanted children, and I might have felt differently if I had been on my own with an unplanned child. There is no knowing how you are going to feel about your baby until he or she is at your mercy. A striking image remains in my mind of another mother in the maternity ward, who could not bear to feed or hold her first baby in spite of tender encouragement from hospital staff and a bewildered husband.

After the cards and flowers from friends and relatives had dwindled to a halt, I was dismayed when some friends, thinking they were paying me a compliment, would say things like, 'You don't look as if you've had a baby at all.' It was as if any mention of the fact that you had become a mother, any celebration beyond the normal courtesies would crack the fragile fabric of your new life. No one tells you that you have to twist your psyche, your health and your money to fit into a society that seems to suffer from a kind of motherism as opposed to sexism, racism or ageism.

Inadequacies in the physical surroundings of our everyday lives struck me more forcefully once I was a mother. Narrow pavements, lack of zebra crossings on dangerous junctions, public toilets with precarious vertical steps onto slippery tiled floors and rooms for nursing mothers not hygenic enough for feeding or changing. Architecture assumed particularly predatory proportions. Lift doors hardly gave me time to get in and out with baby, toddler and shopping.

Driving seemed a lot more hazardous with George in his carry cot on the back seat. Lack of sleep made judging distances between my car and the one in front bewildering. Everything from a juggernaut to a bicycle appeared to be on the road specifically to jangle my nerves and threaten our lives. I am convinced that during the months following the birth I had a stronger sense of danger and self-preservation than before. Even jumping a ditch inspired imaginary applause. This physical cautiousness faded as George grew older, but it was a surprise to the system at the time.

Most of my driving in the early days took me to Leominster Market which took place every Friday. There was a particularly good meat stall, cheese stall and fresh fish shop. Driving in on a sunny day with George on the back seat, a decent night's sleep behind me, and not too many other vehicles on the road, was sometimes invigorating. But queuing at each market stall drove me mad. It was impossible to park the car near the town centre. This meant I had to take two or more trips back and forth with the pushchair laden with bulging plastic bags slung onto the handles. When I took my weight off the handles for a breather, George wasn't heavy enough to prevent it crashing backwards, smashing yoghurts and George's head. It was enough to make me want to fall into the pushchair and have him wheel me to the nearest pub. In fact when I see young mothers now pushing their babies along, it strikes me that they are being pulled by the baby in some way; as if they are sold by the shop along with the pushchair, like an all-in-one bargain kit.

Town planning of the last thirty years rarely suits the needs of anyone, particularly those on a council estate about five miles from the Leominster shopping centre. I would see tightless legs pushing laden prams in the wind and rain back to the estate. There was no crèche, youth club, or launderette on the estate. The council had provided a bus stop with a shelter but public transport, though cheap, wasn't that efficient where we lived. The lack of it made walking along that particular stretch daunting during the dark winter early evenings for those who used it.

Another aspect of physical vulnerability was a greater susceptibility to illness. When I was tired and run down I always seemed to catch whatever George had. If he had a runny nose I would get a bad sore throat and blocked nose. A mild cold in a baby manifests itself with a vengeance in an adult.

My other physical weakness during his first year was my bladder. As George had been delivered by forceps my bladder had become bruised which meant that it wasn't as strong as it should have been. If I sneezed without having been to the toilet within say, an hour, and had had a drink of some kind, the sneeze would make me wet my pants. I found it very difficult to adjust my own toilet training not to mention George's. It is no joke to be wandering round a country town in the pouring rain crossing your legs very hard everytime you sneeze. As time passed my bladder recovered but sometimes, even now, when I'm run down, a sneeze, unexpected, can be humiliating. Nobody had warned me of this possibility, all too common, and I wish they had.

Alcohol can be debilitating enough when you are fit and childless, but when I was a new mother I'm sure it made me more vulnerable to colds and infections. So I gave it up, most of the time, which saved on housekeeping and depression.

Shopping in the local village in the summer was a treat. It fulfilled fantasies of what a mother's life in the country was supposed to be like. After George had his afternoon nap and it was still light, I propped him up in his carry-cot on wheels and walked up the lane to the village, stopping occasionally to talk to a cow or a sheep, who listened startled and polite at this thing on two legs holding up a fart factory in a babygrow who would squeal with delight. The distance was just right for a sunny day and the exercise did help the tiredness. I had a tremendous feeling of me and my baby against the world, until the reality of my own dwindling bank account hit me, and my dependence on my husband and the goodwill of other people, particularly other mothers, made me feel fragile, worried and out of control. I could not make plans for my future as an individual or in the interests of my tiny son. It would have been of some reassurance to me to be able to take out a life insurance pension scheme, not to mention buy a car that started when it was supposed to.

I became bad tempered because I could not get down to my writing, and because I wasn't writing enough I felt that my complaints on the repetition of domestic chores weren't taken seriously. Although domestic work before motherhood had sometimes been an excuse not to write, when I hit a difficult patch, after George, the domestic work was an inescapable reason. I did try to write during George's naps, which were about one and a half hours each, morning and afternoon for his first six months. But there was a knot in my stomach all the time just waiting for him to wake up. Sometimes I would sit in a state of paralysis at my desk just waiting for him to wake; or else I would write in double quick time, hardly pausing to reflect. When the naps became shorter, the problem became more acute. Particularly when he no longer needed a nap in the morning.

As I wrote when he slept I did housework when he was awake. This was manageable until he could crawl, but once he was into everything nothing got done properly. It was unsatisfactory for him because I didn't give him enough attention when hanging out nappies or washing up. If my day was going smoothly and I was calm enough to put the house in order and structure my new-found psyche into working without panic while he slept, someone might drop in. When people drop in in the country they want attention: they have driven some way and want to make an occasion of it. I didn't then know anyone well enough to suggest an alternative day. I believe a lot of exhaustion comes from the sheer strain of never being able to complete anything in one go. Whether it be writing a paragraph, reading a page in a newspaper or drinking a cup of coffee.

Later, once I had learnt to make the most of my time, the panic I first experienced at the prospect of having to stop mid-flow wasn't so bad. But it wasn't easy. I would be pounding way happily at the typewriter and would have to stop mid-inspiration to pick George up from the minder I later employed. This halt to work applies now that I have to pick him and his brother Harry up from school. I call it 'the three o'clock cut off' and it always comes at exactly the wrong moment. But, at least when I've done some writing I feel stronger, emotionally.

But even then, when I was interrupted and it was time to pick George up out of his cot, I'll always remember how my rage would subside when I felt the nuzzle of his furry head between my collar bone and jaw line. So why, I would ask myself, can't I just relax and revel in moments that will pass all too soon? Why do I have these moments of intense anger and worry about not being able to look after myself and George properly? And a sense of missing out and being left behind. I think it was because of my feelings of vulnerability, which are difficult to explain. It always seems to come back to dependency; not so much on my husband, (although that became increasingly true as I worked less), but on the powers and institutions that be. Worries I had before motherhood were nothing compared to the ones that have hit me since. I didn't suffer from post-natal depression, more from rage. Rage because I was and am staggered that nothing has ever been done by society to embrace the incredibly complicated lives of parents, particularly mothers. It is difficult for mothers to join together and change perceptions because the very nature of their existence separates them most of the time. They are not a group in the same way as, say, miners or nurses, which makes it difficult for others to focus on their needs. Also, although mothers in general have the same needs and problems regarding domestic life, they are of course very different as individuals, politically, economically, with different religions. As I gazed over the meadows to the church spire in the distance outlined in the misty sky, I would mutter to myself; 'None of you would exist if it wasn't for mothers.' And give the washing machine a good kick. Rage inspired me to write with a political passion I didn't know I possessed. During George's first two years I wrote a play about a housewife who holds a milkman hostage in order to draw attention to her sense of injustice. But rage can also have a very negative effect and I remember tugging at a sleeve too sharply when helping George on with his coat when I was feeling angry and lonely, then thinking to myself, 'I must never take my feelings out on him. It isn't his fault. He doesn't understand and everything is first time for him.' I would, and still do experience rage that I couldn't leave either of my babies in the pushchair outside a shop for fear of them being taken. I couldn't, and still can't, let them play out of my sight in a public park for the same reason. The danger of a man (in 99 per cent of cases according to any Police Station statistics) destroying a life and kidnapping is always in the background. There are the unexpected dangers or dangers created by sheer stupidity, such as playgrounds with concrete surfaces or unlocked gates onto main roads. Physical dangers created by people are everywhere and put a tremendous strain on the carer or mother.

As my husband now had to earn enough to support the three of us, he was in the classic position of not being able to care for George while I tried to work. Even if I had work I wouldn't have earned enough to support us for the time he took off his work. He did help out, but on an emotional, unpredictable basis rather than a structured one. Even when he did, I butted in to check that George had been given water instead of milk to quench his thirst or that he wasn't choking; or I felt that my husband would misinterpret George's cries that I felt only I understood. The different cries of pain, hunger, tiredness or discomfort; a baby's only means of communication. Once I left George and my husband to their own devices while I travelled to London for a meeting about work. George was eighteen months old and into absolutely everything. I couldn't turn my back for a second. On ringing home to check all was under control, my husband yelled down the phone; 'You must return immediately. He's tipped the nappy bucket full of dirty nappies all over the floor and I haven't been able to finish a phone call since you left.'

I found it increasingly difficult to keep up with myself. I felt as if I was always travelling faster than the speed of light, as the gradual realisation dawned that I had let myself in for an enormous responsibility, the constant pressures and reminders of which ultimately rested with me and would last a lifetime. Even now, whenever I am away from my children, even just for an evening, they are always at the back of my mind. No more getting drunk or throwing caution to the winds. I live with the knowledge that there is a part of me that is always reserved for my children. But I still go through phases of intense anxiety regarding the boys' future. Who would be a suitable guardian? Where and what is safe for them? There is no such place, body, or institution and above all attitude, in our political system that can give any mother reassurance of any kind as far as I can see. Friends and relatives cling onto their own lives and work, fraught with the same anxieties and hardly have the extra energy for extra mouths and emotional, intellectual and practical nurturing that would have to be taken on. The world doesn't care much about defenceless children except in a sentimental way, through charity, or inadequate Social Services.

The local mothers in the country presented a stoic front which made it hard for me to discuss the contradictions of independent urges and maternal ones. Susan, up the lane from us, had a son about the same time I had George. She married into a local family that hired out farm machinery. While she was pregnant she built her house with her husband in her in-laws' farmyard, opposite her mother-in-law's kitchen window. It strikes me hard now, that the minute she became pregnant she put her trust in her in-laws, her house on their land. Soon after she became a mother she did all her husband's paperwork. He was a machine contractor like his father. She also went out on site to calculate and measure which machine was needed for a particular harvest, or lake that had to be dug. She had little to fall back on for security for the future. Seeing mothers in the same economically vulnerable situation as myself underlined my own fragility. I did know mothers who managed lucrative careers in spite of domestic commitments, but they were exceptions. Although I used to drop in on Susan on my walk up the lane with George, and chat lightly about potty training, feeding and village gossip, I soon realised her situation wasn't so difficult, because she could turn to her mother-in-law for free child-minding. I don't know if the mother-in-law wanted this, but anyway there exists the assumption that grandmothers are always happy to be free child-minders and that society is entitled to use them without question, as if they have nothing else they wish to do with their last years. In fact it is my observation that many mothers could not begin to work profitably if it wasn't for grandmothers caring for the grandchildren.

I knew another mother apart from Susan who lived twenty-five miles away on top of a hill miles from anywhere. Her husband is a landed gent with a farm manager and a few hundred acres of Shropshire. We were both bored with the endless repetition of housework and the exhaustion of looking after toddlers and praising their sweet efforts at painting, hide-and-seek or whatever the game of the moment was. Neither of us had any time to ourselves and our conversations were constantly interrupted by our children's very real needs. Permanently bending down is something I shall always remember, to change a nappy, pick up a toy or rescue a child from harming himself. Cleaning up carefully prepared food that had been spat on the floor in disgust was necessary on most days. No job was rewarding. Never being able to sit anywhere except in the kitchen because I always needed a damp cloth, or a mug, or a bottle; and if they were taken to various rooms of the house those rooms had to be cleared up. It is easier to live in the kitchen from a practical point of view when children are under five although it's not good for the mind. If our children were outside playing we had to stay with them because they were bound to be up to something lethal with farm machinery or being kicked or bitten by an animal.

The playgroup I found when George was about eighteen months old and could walk, was ten miles away and functioned for two hours on a Friday morning every week. We ventured there when the car was up to it, George and I, and we had a rude awakening to the inflexibility of the rural English class system. Although babies are equal at playgroup, the mothers would group according to class and chat amongst themselves. Not only that, once the mothers were out of the door, the invites to tea are soon divided up into who isn't who. I was asked to a children's tea party by one aristocrat's wife and I was the only mother in charge of her child. The other childcarers were all nannies. But this was probably rather an extreme example as I did attend other childrens' functions where there were greater varieties of people present. However, it is true that as the children grew older, the classes crossed each other's boundaries even less. Once the aristocrat's child is at a private prep school the village children might be invited up occasionally to share the tennis court or the swimming pool. They are second on the list after the landed gents' children; the last being offspring of professional classes such as lawyers or estate agents. Many rich landowners live in very uncomfortable houses with bad heating and kitchens miles away from playrooms with cold lino on the floor, but nevertheless it was considered a privilege by some people to get a foot in their draughty door. Although the aristocracy in Herefordshire are only glamorised property developers as they are anywhere, owning most of the land when it comes to North Herefordshire, they still think of themselves as being the ones who dictate the complications of rural social life and children are brainwashed by example and behaviour to accept this from a tender age. Being a writer was a great advantage because I didn't fit in anywhere so couldn't be pigeonholed in that prejudiced English way.

As the playgroup was infrequent and unsatisfactory I managed to find a farm labourer's wife who had a three-year-old daughter and was looking for work. She and her husband along with three older children were on family income supplement as her husband earned the National

Farmers Union minimum wage which was not enough to support their family. Even as I employed her I was aware of the fact that my wage to her was very low as it is for most child-minders. Like many caring jobs it is badly paid. A sad reflection on society's unhealthy attitude towards those who work with direct responsibility for children. There was no hope of any financial stability through me either, because I could not always afford her. She was a wonderful child-minder, but I found that whenever I had the choice to leave George with her or not, I was surprised to discover that some days I wanted him to stay with me. I wanted to spend hours walking ten yards up the lane with him, studying sparrows bathing in puddles, and watch his expressions of delight and discovery.

However, there were a few occasions when I couldn't afford the child-minder, or she lost work from me through a domestic problem of her own that made it impossible for her to have George. I would have psyched myself up for my working day only to be let down, at the last minute on a couple of occasions; and then all my feelings of rage, dependency and vulnerability came roaring back. Back to the constant tidying up while my mind was on my work so I didn't listen to George properly. I would cut myself off from him and go into a daze which, of course, made him more demanding. If it was raining there was nowhere to go and nothing to do except play Lego or hide-and-seek in the kitchen, where it was warmest, but where my isolation increased.

When George was about four and a half there was a miraculous moment when I realised he had been playing outside with a friend without crawling through the wire mesh fence into the pond, and I hadn't had to dart all over the place dragging him out of muddy ditches or fish dandelions out of his mouth. Just as children's physical demands decrease, their intellectual, social and emotional ones increase. But this was easier to deal with because George could now talk. His being able to go to the toilet by himself, dress himself, and show me the world through his eyes gave me an enormous sense of release. At last we could communicate without recourse to just weird noises and facial expressions.

It was also about this time that I had to be involved in a rehearsed reading of my play. Although it only took place over a period of a few days I trembled with apprehension wondering how I was going to organise my life without seeming distracted and unprofessional. The work structure meant that the actors read and discussed the play from morning till evening and I would rewrite at night. Fringe theatre is badly funded and there is no provision for childcare rates or amenable hours for mothers. Although I knew that some of the men on the project were fathers, none of them were under the same pressure as I was or worried about their children at the back of their minds. It didn't matter what time they got home. I couldn't pluck up the courage to discuss what I considered to be a communal problem in any workplace – that of the mother or parent worker. I was afraid of losing what little break I had in a notoriously fickle business; which although paying lip service to feminism by employing female playwrights, expressed no curiosity at all in the complications of a working mother's home responsibilities in relation to workplace structures. My husband had to work and didn't have time during the day to help out. Whenever I have had to attend rehearsals or go to meetings I have had to make child-minding arrangements that have left me very nearly out of pocket. I felt if I managed to discuss the problems head on with work colleagues I would be sticking my neck out and making myself vulnerable to even less employment than I already have. Although my work is building up and people appear sympathetic I always feel they don't really understand what I go through and find any discussion of it guilt-making and irritating.

It is interesting that not once has any one of my husband's colleagues asked him how he manages to go to meetings, rehearsals and evening functions when he has a family that has to be protected for at least the next fifteen years. It is completely taken for granted that he is free to come and go as he pleases without any extra expense or any need for extra child-minding allowance. If he had an allowance to pay me that would be perfectly acceptable to me as so much of my time when he is away consists of physical drudgery rather than productive hours playing with the children.

I read somewhere that the Chinese have nurseries and laundries at places of work so that parents can take children under five to the factory, eat meals with them and at the same time get the washing done. The family is given tea at the workplace so that the parents can give the children their undivided attention at home in the evening, instead of tearing around cooking, shopping, and shoving things in and out of the washing machine. Being able to have meals, check on the children and cuddle them at work, would dispel anxieties about abandonment from both the parents' and the child's point of view.

One of the ways I found to cut down on menial tasks, whether I was working or not, was to cook just one evening meal at six-thirty – instead of cooking one meal for the children and another later on for us. Cooking the children's meal, putting them to bed (a major war in itself), clearing up their supper things, cooking a new meal for us, took up four hours of the evening and I was lucky if I made it in time to sit down for the ten o'clock news. 'Dinner' for grown-ups is a legacy from the Victorian and Edwardian eras when slave-waged servants did all the work and is ludicrously impractical for modern parents with no domestic help. I have also always felt a lot healthier for eating earlier. If my husband misses the evening meal then he doesn't get any. He has to cook it himself. I can't bear the feeling that I should run different meal sittings like British Rail. Also, once children are about seven they go to bed later, so giving each other undivided attention over a candlelit chop is not possible. With an early evening meal there is a lot more of the the evening left for the parents to give each other attention if they want to.

In spite of many pleasurable times in the country I felt cut off and the phone hardly ever rang. Work connections bothered to keep in contact less and less. A kind of apathy set in and nothing changed much except the seasons. We left the country for work reasons just as George was due to start primary school. We have a large London garden, but Harry would like a dog and they would both like to have adventures in woods and go for bicycle rides.

Sometimes I miss being thrown back into the romantic isolation of the country. London life is narrow in a different way. I see much of people doing the same kind of work as I do. My perceptions and views aren't challenged as they were in the country, meeting people with totally different historical and anthropological backgrounds. But it is easy to romanticise in retrospect. In the city everything is made by people. In the country, the elements, the distances and the history the country is steeped in controls the people. As does the weather.

As I set about the domestic routines of family life I reflect a great deal on the different perceptions motherhood has given me. One of them is that mothers possess a kind of constructive anarchy. They constantly do each other favours in society that only judges people by their wage: picking each other's children up from school, for example, in order to be able to stay longer at work. This aspect of mutual positive help puts mothers who do it in one class; but an underclass because of society's refusal to recognise the fact that it is work.

Mothers and the knowledge and perceptions they have through motherhood are exploited for money and for political ambition of other people, rarely the mothers. Mothers know quicker than anyone else what is needed, what is unsatisfactory, and what works in the local community, and better than any journalist or politician. The discussions that take place in a school playground are more informed than any that go on in Parliament as regards the social conditions of society. This particularly hits me when I watch the news on television. There is hardly ever news or statistics concerning mothers, their unemployment figures, their average income, what they are doing while their menfolk fight wars, statistics on domestic violence. Some of these aspects may be touched on, occasionally, but only in a token way. Mothers in our society are outsiders. News is never female, even when read by a female newscaster. Exploitation of mothers in the workforce and home is not reported on regularly such as, say, nurses' pay or miners'.

At the moment mothers can lose their innate sense of democracy once they become paid achievers in order to survive. Right-wing female politicians and career women who, though passionate about their own careers and their right not to be economically and sexually vulnerable, don't seem to do anything about female vulnerability for the rest of the female population. This attitude prevails amongst childless workers as well. Whereas childless folk and parents in different kinds of jobs will support anti-racism, anti-sexism, anti-ageism and promote Gay Rights, it doesn't seem to have occurred to most to make sure that work structures don't prejudice a mother's chances of decent pay and flexible hours. Which is curious when you think everyone in the world has had, or still has, a mother. It's as if no one has ever been able to see their own mother as a human being, so great has been the cover-up of what most mothers really feel, need and perceive.

Being a mother has made me understand the frailties and confusions of other people because I see the process of two growing lives. For me it is important to have children and fight injustices that men and women face, rather than be defeated by the exploitation that motherhood can but needn't bring, and deny the intense desire to bear and love children. My sons have taught me an invaluable lesson on my own, and other people's, vulnerability. And for that at the very least I shall always love them more than anyone else.

Whilst writing the first draft of this essay the bathroom ceiling fell.in and I had a nightmare time clearing up and arranging repairs. Whilst writing the second draft the kitchen ceiling fell in, my husband wrote the car off and my husband also wrote the fridge off by piercing a gas pipe in the fridge with a hammer whilst trying to be useful defrosting it. That is the sort of writing he does when away from the typewriter. This writing off of essential equipment left me depressed and even more exhausted. George said to me in the car yesterday, out of the blue; 'Mum, you know when you're horrible?' 'When?' I said in panic. Fondly thinking I disguised my bad moods quite well most of the time. 'Well, when you are,' said George. 'Yes?' I said in a slightly high-pitched voice. 'Well Mum, why can't you behave more like the mothers in the ads sometimes?'

Girls
Can't Be Professors, Mummy

Last week as I was washing up while my daughter had her bath, I happened to hear some of the radio programme 'In Business' discussing the lack of women in top management. The contributor rightly recognised that few women would reach the top unless more reached middle management and, of course, the move into middle management coincides with the time when women are most likely to be having children. On the programme were two young women: one had two small children, the other was married, but had yet to start her family. Both sounded utterly confident that it was possible to combine demanding careers with having children. The one who already had children had a full-time nanny and a husband who, she claimed, shared domestic responsibilities equally (although we were only told about his cooking abilities). It all sounded so easy! Provided women can afford and have access to 'full-time' childcare and have a helpful husband or partner, they can, then, have their cake and eat it.

My uneasiness was not so much about wanting one's cake and eating it, but about the lack of questioning, the nature of the cake, and irritation (and probably envy) that it could seem so simple. I too am immensely privileged to have a job which I enjoy and which pays well, and a partner who shares more childcare than many fathers do. (Of course, none of these things should be a privilege.) When my daughter, now aged eight years old, was very young, I could afford to take nine months maternity leave (and even in my job most of that was *un*paid) and then employ a nanny (after much thought, but more of that later) until she was old enough to go to the nursery at the university where I worked. I was in my late thirties when my daughter was born, I had been promoted while I was pregnant (although they didn't know at the time – had they done so, I wonder if I would have been) and this year was promoted again to become a head of department (the only woman in that position in my college). So on the face of it, I am an example of the successful woman being described on that programme and shouldn't have had any major difficulties or dilemmas. But I did, and still do, and it is these I want to write about and share. For while I had the financial resources to buy myself out of some of the major problems facing many mothers, the 'solutions' I bought were not unproblematic, and those dilemmas I continue to struggle with raise issues which go far beyond more childcare provision, vital though that is.

I know other feminists struggle with these dilemmas too but in the seventies they did not appear very visibly on feminist agendas. Indeed, the reaction of some of my feminist friends to the news that I was going to have a baby seemed to me to be one of dismay – even of letting the side down – especially from those who had had children at a much younger age and before the re-emergence of the women's movement; someone in my position 'should have known better'. I certainly found it puzzling (and still do) as to why I felt unable to talk with the women's group of which I'd been part for over five years about how I felt about being a mother and, subsequently, how I was going to continue in the job I still wanted to do. I notice I have already described myself as '*being* a mother' and that it seems to me is from where some of the dilemmas come.

One of the abiding features of motherhood is that it is a state of being and a very preoccupying state at that. I really do mean state and I really do mean abiding. I do not mean a 'role' which implies something entailing choice and something which is played for a finite time. Neither do I mean work – although in much of my writing I have drawn attention to the ways in which caring for children *is* work. It is not work, however, in the sense that the child is the end product. Although I've never believed, as some psychologists have asserted, that babies arrived like blank sheets upon which the environment, including parents, could inscribe, thus determining the form of the adult personality, aptitudes and intellect, I was still surprised at just how complete a person a baby actually is. Dienka arrived not only with a personality with likes and dislikes that were revealed very quickly, but, apparently, with a wealth of experience. Part of this was a time in some previous existence when she believed she was a boy, for until she was three, she was convinced – and I've since discovered it's not an uncommon conviction in children – boys had previously been girls and vice versa. How that fits into theories of gender formation goodness knows, except as further evidence that there is male and female in all of us.

That being so, baby and childcare manuals seem to me to be quite mistaken in implying mothers can produce certain kinds of children with certain kinds of aptitudes. I think we can *encourage* children to develop their potential (or not to) in particular ways, with more or less respect and concern for other people. We certainly influence the kind of moral values to which they ascribe, but the material with which we work is not nearly as 'raw' as some of the experts would have us believe. Whatever else motherhood is, it is not something which you take on or do on top of everything else: it seems to alter every layer of one's being and therefore once embarked upon cannot be completely discarded. Even Mrs Thatcher recognised this when she described her thoughts as she looked at her new-born twins: 'I'm not going to be overcome by this,' and immediately registered for her Bar finals and employed a nanny.[1] Similarly, when I was pregnant, I was advised by a woman senior civil servant with whom I was working at the time to get back to work as soon as possible after my baby was born, 'even though all your instincts will tell you to stay at home'. (She had had five children.) So that's no great revelation, but for me one of the most important consequences of becoming a mother is that I have lost the opportunity, privilege, ability, or whatever, to be completely single-minded. Maybe that should not matter to me – after all, being overcome by a tiny baby had its immensely pleasurable aspects – but it does, although quite why it matters is unclear.

It may be to do with the undisciplined way in which I work and my need to get totally immersed in a subject before writing about it and then writing almost continuously for several days. At least during vacations I could do this before Dienka arrived but now my time for reading and writing is not so open-ended. I have to time-table chunks of time (including getting up very early in the morning which does not come easily to me) and try and hold on to ideas over the gaps when other demands are made on my time and attention. Constant breaking off and trying to pick up the threads of an argument is not very conducive to developing a line of thought, let alone an analysis. But this is only one of the many consequences of the fragmentation of women's time, not only because we live in increasingly fragmented societies in the West which affects both men and women, but also because it is *women* who are responsible for helping others survive this fragmentation. In Laura Balbo's words, women 'are kept busy at this piecing and patching, hardworking and resourceful, in charge of the well-being of those who depend upon them and feeling responsible when they fail.'[2]

Certainly motherhood has been an experience which has made me aware of time in many different ways. In particular how much women's time is taken for granted so that there is little concordance between the way time is structured in the so-called public world and the rhythm of time associated with caring for a young child. When struggling to get Dienka to school on time (throughout her time at infant school I was one of 'the late mothers'), I remembered Adrienne Rich's description of a summer holiday spent in Vermont with her three sons. She described how she fell into what she called 'a delicious and sinful rhythm' when they 'ate nearly all meals outdoors, hand-to-mouth, we lived half-naked, stayed up to watch bats and stars and fire-flies, read and told stories, slept late . . . At night they fell asleep without murmur and I stayed up reading and writing as I had when a student, till the early morning hours. I remember thinking; this is what living with children could be – without school hours, fixed routines, naps, the conflict of being both mother and wife with no room for being simply, myself.'[3] In some ways the very early weeks of Dienka's life felt like that and they were a wonderful contrast to the routines and endless deadlines of the Cabinet Office which I had just left. What was very clear in the advice we new mothers were given at the ante-natal classes and in the childcare manuals was that such behaviour could only be condoned for the first six weeks. After that it was indeed sinful to neglect the housework and routines of one's husband and *his* work.

Of course, like most women, I knew already that our time was accorded less importance both within the family and outside, not least because I had grown up in a family where the divisions of responsibilities between my parents was very 'traditional'. I was very well aware of the many ways in which my mother's time was presumed to be at the disposal of my father. For example, he came home for lunch every day and my mother not only had to prepare it but had to *be* there. I liked her to be at home too when I came home from school for tea, but she was not, on the afternoons when she worked in my father's office (and *I* got the tea ready). A lot of my work in the 1970s both as a feminist and as an academic had been based around challenging marriage as a profoundly unequal relationship reinforced by a whole panoply of State policies and there's no doubt that as much of this was informed by the experience of my parents' marriage as by my more academic research. This was particularly so because my mother as well as my father described their marriage as a 'good' one. I have avoided marriage and do not live all the time with my daughter's father, but having stayed clear of the legal trappings of marriage, I cannot claim to have missed all or even most of the pitfalls. Certainly I was apprehensive that having a child might make me more dependent on her father than I wanted to be, and I am sure the decision not to have a second child was in part, at least, because I doubted my ability to retain the degree of autonomy I had struggled so hard to acquire.

As Alice Walker has written explaining why she had one child: 'with one you can move; with more than one you're a sitting duck'.[4] Certainly when confronted (and I choose that word deliberately) with the possibility of having another child, I was very frightened by the prospect of being a 'sitting duck'. Exactly why, I do not fully understand and certainly can't put my feelings into words. Even if I could, I would not include them here because I would prefer that my daughter learned about that particular dilemma from me at a time of her choosing (if she does so choose) rather than because of chancing to read this book. All I will say are two things: first, that I realised how precarious my financial situation would have rapidly become had I wanted another child *and* had wanted to take as much maternity leave as I'd taken (and felt I needed) the first time. I had used up my savings, and unpaid leave would have meant total dependence on Dienka's father for I could not see how I would qualify for any social security beyond maternity benefit (and now that is less than it was when I had Dienka). I certainly would not have been entitled to anything had I lived with him, but on the other hand I did not want to manage two young children on my own. So, my feelings about being a mother are also entangled with my feelings about being dependent, one important dimension of this being the economic one, but that is by no means the only one.

Second, being a mother is also about *having* a dependent. While I believe relationships between adults should not be ones of structured inequality in which one (the woman in a heterosexual couple) is forced to be dependent on the other, the relationship between mother and child starts off by being a profoundly unequal one. I don't see how it could be otherwise. A baby, a small child *and* older children all need at least one adult who is preoccupied with their welfare, who gives their needs priority and who organises their lives to take account of them and, if necessary, can be relied upon to drop everything else in a crisis to provide or mobilise whatever support is needed. While a child's needs change as she or he gets older and the preoccupation will have to manifest itself differently, it is, nevertheless, necessary. Certainly, when they are small babies, their lives literally depend on just this support. How then do mothers (or the child's principal caretaker) make room for other things they want to do, and how is a balance to be struck? That's one of the questions that I still struggle with because my identity was so bound up with my career long before

Dienka arrived on the scene and it still is, although being a mother is now also part of it.

My own mother's experiences do not help much here except to convince me that it is in no one's interest not to have some regard for oneself as well as for others, and that the restrictions on her time were as much to do with being a wife as with being a mother. My mother did not return to her work as a physiotherapist until my brother and I were adult. However, she did help my father with his business while we were children. That was acceptable to him for it was just another way in which she put her time at his disposal. Tragically, no sooner had she become established back in the work she so enjoyed than she discovered she had multiple sclerosis; she died six years later. I found among her papers a letter from the local hospital regretting that she had, after all, not been able to accept a part-time post as physiotherapist. The letter had been written twenty years earlier and dated from the time when my brother went to boarding school and my mother started to work for my father. I'll never know why she kept that letter all those years, for she had kept very few letters that long, and the others I found were obviously significant. Until that time, I had no idea that she had actually tried to take up physio-therapy again while we were children, although we had talked about the problems involved in combining a career and family.

I do know that she derived little pleasure from the work in my father's office and devised many strategies to limit the range of tasks she was expected to do. (I only realised that years afterwards. I think we are very slow to acknowledge and therefore to recognise the forms of resistance women adopt to limit the extent of incorporation into their hus-band's jobs.) So the experience of my mother being at home full time, as I observed it, meant that, in addition to being more readily available to meet the demands my brother and I made on her, my father was able to depend on her in the sense of making demands on her time and attention much more than if she had been involved either in paid work of her own choosing or some other activity outside of the home. So the model of mothering I had grown up with *and* found very comfortable as a child was too bound up with being a 'good' wife and was not one I wanted to follow. But I wasn't rejecting it because I thought my mother had been a bad mother – on the contrary.

So what did I want? One possibility is to share the responsibility for caring for and about children with other committed adults. But, although I wanted to share, I found I certainly did not want to share equally. No doubt this is partly because I am my mother's daughter and she had provided most of the care and I had found this a very positive experience. Also, I think that if I had only wanted partial responsibility for a child then I did not need to have a child myself; children were already a small part of my life at the time we decided to have Dienka. In any case, doesn't being a mother or at least a 'good' mother in our society now mean being the primary caretaker? Such a definition of a 'good' mother holds many dangers both for mothers and for children, I believe. It seems to me too much is loaded on to the mother/child relationship and too little heed is paid to relationships children may have with other caring adults.

At the end of my maternity leave, when it was time to move back to Bristol because that's where my job then was (I had been living in London with Dienka's father when she was born for I had been on secondment from my university post), it would have been possible to leave her in London, spend the week in Bristol, and travel back to London at weekends. The childcare arrangements I made in Bristol could have been made in London but I didn't want to be away from her as much as that. I felt I would have been reducing the opportunity of getting to know her, as she developed so rapidly, and I didn't want to miss that. Instead, we both spent the week in Bristol and returned together to London at the weekends to join her father and his three older children from his first marriage. One of my colleagues, however, *was* able to make that arrangement and I found myself feeling rather disapproving of her. I felt even more critical when she left her two-year-old daughter for six weeks to go abroad – but why did I feel like this? Is it because we are so unsure of what we are doing that if someone else manages it differently, it's very threatening; or because we might be labelled by others a 'bad' mother, or worse, because we are not living up to what *we* think a 'good' mother is?

While I know what sharing material resources means, I do not really know what I want in terms of sharing care because, when it came to it, I didn't and still don't want to give up being the primary carer – although I've never wanted sole responsibility. I was so preoccupied with Dienka when she was a baby that I had a writing block for over two years. It wasn't until I went away for a week to Canada to speak at a conference that I broke the block. Although I went feeling very guilty, I came back feeling positive about my work and discovered that Dienka had been perfectly happy in my absence, although she was, gratifyingly, very pleased to see me again. And so I was able to disengage myself sufficiently to write a chapter for a book in two weeks flat (much to the relief of the editor!). I still have to wait until she is asleep or out of the house before I can write. I cannot disengage myself from her in the way her father can when she is around, which is what I think my daughter means when she says, 'The trouble with Daddy is he does not take any notice of me.' He actually takes a lot of notice of her, but he *can* switch off in her presence.

Another set of contradictions surrounds paying for child-care. I thought long and hard about the arrangements I should make when my maternity leave was over. The university nursery only took children when they were at least two years old, so that wasn't a possibility in the first instance. Although women who employ nannies have a bad name, I was not, and still am not, convinced that nannies are necessarily any more exploited than child-minders, although the opportunities for exploitation are greater because childcare can extend into domestic work so much more easily. I certainly felt it was easier for *me* to have Dienka looked after at home rather than for me to need to be sufficiently well organised to take her somewhere else each day. In addition, I was home late sometimes and felt it would be easier to negotiate extra hours with someone living at home than with a child-minder and/or arrange for someone else to fetch her and put her to bed. It *is* possible to have a contract that sets out the hours and boundaries of the job and to pay a proper rate including extra for overtime. As I was paying half my post-tax income for Dienka to be looked after for what amounted to half her waking hours for five days a week, I don't take kindly to the accusation that I was an exploitative employer, although there is no getting away from the fact that I *was* an employer, and that is not an equal relationship. There are contradictions in the situation facing women who want to return to their jobs where there is no alternative to purchasing private care in the marketplace, but what strategy is 'ideologically sound'? What does a self-respecting feminist do in this un-reconstructed world?

On the other hand, nursery provision had its contradictions too. The university nursery I used was only supported by the university to the extent of providing the building rent-free. All other expenses associated with the building, plus staff and equipment costs, had to be met by the parents using the nursery. There were considerable pressures not to pay staff much more than the minimum rate. Parents also had to give some of their time to managing the nursery; we hadn't escaped from being an employer albeit a collective one. Parents did not necessarily agree amongst themselves, let alone with the staff, about how the nursery should be run. Most parents did not object to the girls' pegs being identified by labels with different flowers while the boy's labels had toy engines, boats, etc. A trivial example, perhaps, but indicative of the issues. Not everyone wanted or cared about non-sexist and non-racist games, books, equipment, etc. Trained nursery staff will have been taught from textbooks which implicitly or explicitly teach that it is better for mothers to be at home with their children. Many, if not most of the young women attracted to train to work as a nursery nurse or nanny for that matter are likely to have very 'traditional' ideas about childcare and gender roles which are reinforced by their training. They are therefore doing a job they would not want someone to do for them (or at this stage of their lives they think they wouldn't).

On a more practical level, care outside the home has its problems, one of which is that it's of no use if the child is not well enough to use it. Illness, which is of its nature unpredictable, is very problematic and it seems to me that the answer lies mainly in employers and the State being much more supportive (in every sense making sure that there are no financial losses incurred) when an adult has to take time off to look after a sick child. The demand for more childcare provision in the form of nurseries is not a straightforward one and does not necessarily avoid all the pitfalls of private care in the home.

Some of the problems encountered in the nursery carry over to the schools. Indeed, because of the more restricted hours, I found childcare for my daughter once she was at primary school more problematic. The structure of the education system – the shorter length of the school day which did not coincide with my working day, the lack of flexibility about the time at which children can arrive at school and the promptness with which they must be picked up, the announcement of in-service training days at very short notice, are telling examples of the way in which mothers' time is completely taken for granted. (While writing this piece, I've received a letter saying the school will be closed for two days in a fortnight's time.)

Avon, the local education authority in which I live,

makes no after-school play provision, but the parents at some schools, particularly in the inner city areas, have got together and have *created* after-school play provision. My daughter's school has a scheme that is shared with a neighbouring school. However, it staggers from crisis to crisis as one bit of funding runs out and others have to be found. Because of the insecure financial base, it is impossible to offer the play-workers any security so they not surprisingly come and go more rapidly than is desirable. The parents using the scheme, many of whom are lone mothers, do so because we have jobs, but on top of this and our family responsibilities, we are expected to find time to manage these schemes as well as to raise funds. So the cost of the after-school play provision my daughter enjoys is not only measured in terms of money but also in terms of *time*, something which working parents, especially mothers with small children, have very little to spare. While I do not think it wrong that parents should take some responsibility for provision of this kind and it seems highly desirable we should have some say in it, I do not think that it should rest entirely on our shoulders. That it does is a reflection of the fact that as a society we increasingly regard children as the *sole* responsibility of their parents (and mothers, in particular).

This became very explicit when last year Avon seriously considered a proposal to move to a so-called continental school day which would have meant school finishing at one o'clock or thereabouts. Only children entitled to free meals would be provided with lunch. The proposal arose from the problem of providing and paying for supervision during the lunch break, as well as from pressure to cut back on the cost of the school meal service. 'Responsible' parents, councillors told us, would make sure that they would be at home when their children finished school. Fortunately, parents and teachers alike made their opposition to the idea very clear and, the education committee, having made a commitment to consult *and* listen to parents, found it difficult to go ahead with the proposals – but I doubt whether the idea is dead and buried. If schools could be used for other activities when formal teaching ended, and there was adequate supervision, then a continental school day would be an attractive idea (and in practice on the continent there *is* alternative provision made for children – it is *not* assumed they will all go home to their mothers). Sadly, this is not on the agenda in this country.

While I am still unclear about how much and in what ways I really want to share responsibilities for caring within the family (and I know that begs a lot of questions I've not addressed), I think I am much clearer about ways in which the wider community could recognise and, then, meet the needs of mothers and children. For example, it very quickly became clear after Dienka was born that the view 'a mother's place is in the home' literally means just that. Travelling around with babies and young children is difficult because so many public places and public transport are so unwelcoming to children. I've never had a car so I rely heavily on buses and trains as well as walking. Latterly, I bought myself out of the problem by taking taxis and this involved not only being able to afford to do so, but also feeling free to do so.

I was not surprised to read that a recent survey found that men able to claim business expenses claimed far more than women in equivalent positions and this was particularly noticeable with respect to taxis. We walk or use public transport because *we* do not place as much value on our time as men do on theirs. Folding buggies were a wonderful invention, but even so, it is difficult to struggle on and off buses and underground trains with them. Thank goodness the minibuses, which have resulted from privatising bus services and which are increasingly replacing larger buses with space for storing a buggy and a conductor to help, were not around when Dienka was small. Even then I don't think I would have managed two little ones plus shopping. They are not designed for anyone struggling with shopping and a young child or anyone who is not able-bodied. As for the underground system – the level of concern for travellers with babies and toddlers begins and ends with the unrealistic exhortation to fold all buggies before using an escalator.

If men had to travel with children in buggies on public transport as often as they had to carry briefcases, I suspect they would have devised a rather different transport system and invented escalators and steps on which it was possible to take children in buggies easily. I also found that most people were in too much of a hurry to help as well: middle-aged women were the most likely to help. I read with envy recently that French railways have long-distance trains with an entire coach given over to children's play. Most of the time Dienka was very 'good' on our weekend train journeys between Bristol and London and certainly the train was much more enjoyable and easier than a coach, especially when it was not too crowded, but how much easier and how much more fun it would have been if there had been play facilities, too. (A sticky, tired child on a crowded train is no fun for anyone.) Instead, British Rail have invested in facilities for the businessman.

The road planners do no better by making pedestrians accommodate themselves to the car, and not the other way around. The priority given to the private car makes roads *and* pavements dangerous for other users, thus making children dependent on an escort for longer. In situations where cars and pedestrians are separated, the latter have to contend with underpasses, pedestrian bridges, etc., designed by people who have never had to use them or certainly not with children and/or shopping in tow. Even shopping, which is presumed to be a woman's activity, has to be done in an environment that is unsympathetic to mothers' needs and again presumes that women's time is not valuable. I found shopping in city centres difficult not just because of the lack of provision for changing and feeding babies, but also because of the layout of department stores. Because men's time is considered more valuable than women's, the goods they are likely to purchase are to be found on the ground floor. Only recently, for example, have Marks and Spencer's started putting babies and toddlers clothes on the ground floor.

I had begun to be aware of what a difficult environment we had created for anyone who was not able-bodied in the late 1960s, when my mother had become increasingly handicapped by mutliple sclerosis. Having Dienka really brought home to me that measured in terms of mobility, having a baby, or a small child, is like being disabled. Indeed, I read a survey recently which included women with children among those having 'a personal mobility problem'. That is a very sad comment on our society which after all provides those whose time and work is valued with the means to be mobile, even if this means providing cars with chauffeurs available at any time. There is a lot of work to be done by feminists and others in thinking about how we could create an environment which is welcoming to children, positively. One thing is very clear, extending ownership of the private car is *no* solution. On the contrary, it makes the problems worse.

The planners of transport, public spaces and amenities do not take account of mothers' and children's needs, neither do employers. If they do, it is in return for less pay, loss of promotion prospects, etc. I have been very fortunate in having a job which has far more flexibility than many, and when I have had to take time off to look after Dienka when she was unwell (so far a rare occurrence, fortunately), I have not had to worry about losing money. Lectures and classes can be rearranged and I have found my students (most of whom are women, although only a minority have children) understanding. More important, I have always had both a head of department who was sympathetic and other women colleagues who also had young children. Nevertheless, there are many pressures operating which make it hard to combine motherhood with being a full-time academic because, although the structure is less formal and less explicit than in many jobs, the demands made on our time presume we do *not* have responsibility for childcare (and often that we have the services of a wife). Had I had a child earlier in my career it would have been *much* harder to resist some of these pressures.

I do not remember much about my first year back in my job after maternity leave except that I was tired all the time, but did not realise just *how* tired until later. If I had heeded the advice of my former colleague in the Cabinet Office and returned to work earlier, I would have needed *more* than full-time help to cope with the broken nights, etc., to avoid being even more tired. Even so, if I had not had ten years of teaching, a recent year's study leave, and experience of the world inside central government on which to draw, I would have found it very difficult to meet my teaching commitments. Although my colleagues, in general, have always been sympathetic to those with small children, they certainly did not make any concessions to me in that first year back. In fact, the administrative load I carried was increased that year. Fortunately, the pressure (both self-imposed as well as from outside) to publish, attend conferences, etc., was reduced for the time being: I had been promoted. I was also in a stronger negotiating position over time-tabling my teaching, the times of staff meetings, etc. Indeed, because I chaired the meetings, I could at least endeavour to make sure they finished on time. The carelessness about starting and finishing meetings promptly is an example of how little value we place on each other's time. Moreover, I noted that those male colleagues who were most disapproving of mothers with small children working full-time were the first to arrange an extra meeting *starting* at 5 p.m. Here I felt in a double bind. On the one hand I wanted to be and to show that I was a responsible, caring mother, who made sure she was at home for tea, bath-time, and bedtime story (which I enjoy and hate missing) but, on the other hand, I also wanted to show I could still do the job 'properly'. I therefore had very mixed feelings when one of my senior colleagues in the Faculty commented on how I appeared not to let having a child interfere with my work – was that praise or criticism?

Those pressures are far worse now than they were ten years ago. Teaching loads are higher, the pressure to publish and establish a reputation by attending and giving papers at conferences (preferably abroad) are very great. With half of all women in academic posts now being on fixed-term contracts (twice the proportion of men), being considered 'unproductive' for even a short time can, quite literally, cost you your job. Having sat in on discussions about promotion, I have heard for myself how working evenings and long hours over weekends in the laboratory, for example, are used as evidence of commendable commitment to the work. That cannot be done as a parent unless one has considerable help with domestic and child-care responsibilities – or a wife. Working mothers have to anticipate and negotiate every minute of extra time on the job. This means relying on several sources of childcare. For example, the after-school play scheme I've already mentioned has to leave the school premises very promptly at 5.30 p.m. because the cleaners and the caretaker want to finish *their* work on time. As a result, any possibility of a seminar or meeting running over time, or transport running late, has to be allowed for, and arrangements have to be made for someone else to take over. When the play scheme finishes, many mothers are in a similar position. Arranging childcare becomes a perpetual juggling act and it is crucial to have people you can call on to help at very short notice.

I have, very recently, changed my job and no longer work only a ten-minute cycle ride from my home. Instead, eighty miles separates home from work and I am away from home one or two nights a week. At the moment Dienka's father looks after her when I am away, but when that is no longer possible, I shall have to think again – at the time of writing I have not decided what arrangements I shall make. This may not seem an ideal situation — my life is now more fragmented — but had I decided immediately to move house to be closer to my job (assuming I could afford to do so), I would have been starting a new and more demanding job at the same time as settling Dienka into a new home, new school, new neighbourhood. I did not feel I had the emotional resources to do all of that at once, especially without a local supportive network. Again, men do not usually have to consider that aspect of caring for children when they change jobs and location. They may postpone a move because of the disruption to a child's education, but not much more.

I had to think long and hard about whether or not to change my job not just in terms of potential job satisfaction but also in terms of whether I *and* Dienka could manage the necessary domestic changes. It's early days yet and there are times, especially when Dienka is feeling under the weather, that I wonder whether I was wise. However, there are also advantages. Because I am away from home for part of the week, for the first time in ten years I have one or two evenings a week guaranteed to be completely free of domestic responsibilities. It seems to me that men, as a matter of course, create structures (in time and space) to give themselves just that kind of freedom — indeed, women as wives and/or secretaries and so on, help them to create these structures and maintain the boundaries between their 'work' and their 'family'. It is easier for men because their jobs impose a *legitimate* structure on their lives which excuses them from the demands of childcare and indeed caring for adults. Not so for women: they must combine the two in a way that does not harm their children and, it is assumed, that this can only be done by taking no account of *their* own needs and wishes. It is as if, almost by definition, a mother who considers herself must be a less caring (careless?) mother.

Nevertheless, the demands of some jobs, as they are

currently defined, are such that it is not possible to satisfactorily balance the two. I do not believe I could have done my present job when Dienka was much younger; I would have had neither the physical nor emotional resources, quite apart from not having the time. For me, that raises questions about the way we structure employment, not just in terms of its location and the length of the working day, although these are very important, but also in terms of hierarchies of responsibilities. Perhaps if responsibilities and decision-making were more widely diffused throughout organisations, then so-called senior jobs would be less burdensome and less greedy of their incumbents' time and attention. Or, if that is not the case then we need to examine at what stage in life people move into more demanding jobs.

As I started by saying, the first crucial moves coincide with the time when women are most likely to be very absorbed in childcare – that certainly suits men, but does that have to be the case because of the intrinsic nature of the work? Similarly, with more and more emphasis on early retirement (I have recently received a letter to the effect that I am now old enough to bid for early retirement in three years' time!), women who have become more interested in their paid work after their children have become less dependent on them, increasingly find that they have just got started when the pressure is on them to leave and make way for a younger person (man). These are just other examples of the lack of congruence between the demands *and* needs of children, and the demands of paid work. As a feminist, I would like to see the world of employment adjusted to meet the needs of children and those who care for them instead of having to walk a tightrope between the two. For a start, mothers' time – for ourselves as well as for our children – *must* be acknowledged and more highly valued.

Notes

1. Beatrix Campbell, *The Iron Ladies*, Virago Press, 1987, p. 239.
2. Laura Balbo, 'Crazy Quilts: rethinking the Welfare State debate from a woman's point of view' in *Women and the State* ed. Anne Showstack Sassoon, Hutchinson, 1987, p. 66.
3. Adrienne Rich, *Of Woman Born*, Virago, 1977, p. 194.
4. Alice Walker, 'One Child of One's Own' in *In Search of Our Mother's Gardens*, Women's Press, 1984, p. 363.

Rahila Gupta

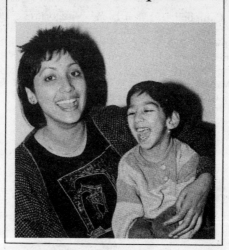

Giving Birth Again

One of the most memorable lines from the film *Rosa* (directed by Margaretha Von Trotta) on Rosa Luxemburg's life is when she expresses a desire to have children and her lover dissuades her with, 'Children teach you fear.' Although I saw the film long after my pregnancy, it encapsulated a vaguely sensed and semi-articulated feeling that surfaced after the initial euphoria of a successful conception. Even before my son was born, I had stopped taking risks. I had become cautious about taking a frontline position at a demonstration or march in case I got caught up in a scuffle with the police. I resented family and friends for the consideration showed to me, my diet, my life-style merely because I was a carrier of something more precious. I resented myself for doing the same. The care you take of your body during pregnancy is the first point of departure from feminist principles. You assume importance through your function rather than who you are as an individual. A woman's health should be important *per se* instead of being subordinated to the health of a child because, historically, that is what we have always done and so colluded in our own exploitation. We have had secondary importance as appendages rather than in our own right. And here I was, aware of these factors and unable to detach myself from a sense of my own preciousness.

A friend of mine remarked on how the process had turned her into a reactionary, unconsciously. She had begun home improvements during pregnancy and had become extremely sceptical of the local education facilities before her daughter had even left the hospital. Attempting to put in double glazing or central heating if you can afford it represents the same shift in focus. Why is the comfort of the newcomer more important than your own? And if your work consists of rehousing women and children who live in damp housing with bare minimum protection against winter the contradictions become even more painful.

I had visualised my life after pregnancy very much in feminist terms. I was committed to two people sharing childcare, especially in a heterosexual relationship. After all, my partner and I had shared domestic chores right from the start. However, early in my pregnancy, I had been made redundant when the voluntary organisation, whose magazine I edited, lost its funding. I found temporary work with a feminist newspaper, but that hardly represented the kind of economic stability from which I could negotiate my freedom. While feminism provided a framework for the understanding of women's oppression in economic, social and political terms, it also placed great emphasis on life-style politics (like all political and religious philosophies). Feminism's rallying slogan, 'The personal is political' made it doubly imperative for the individual woman to change her domestic practice as a sign of her commitment to her political beliefs. So, although I understood that the forces that affected my domestic situation were larger than myself, my feminist politics obliged me to consider personal choices that I should be making to liberate myself from domestic oppression. But the compromises were these – my partner's earning capacity was enough to sustain a comfortable life-style for all of us. Had I got a part-time job and asked him to work part-time, our incomes would not have allowed for the same comfort. In addition there were two principles in conflict. On principle I would not work in the commercial sector because that would be death to my politics. That narrowing down of the field, further aggravated by part-time availability, meant that there were few job options left. The other, the principle of truly shared childcare – the undoing of that stranglehold that feminists had identified as the first barrier to self-determination – simply went out of the window.

Many feminists live with these pressures. It may be argued that I am being a purist, and that in making feminism appear so rigorous, I am excluding other women from joining its ranks. But in these days of designer feminism, when women's glossy magazines have undermined the revolutionary potential of feminism by parading an endless series of high-powered, successful women as if that were all feminism had set out to achieve, it is important to reinforce the original focus. Of course, there are tremendous difficulties, considering that Thatcherism has forced us on the defensive, protecting the few gains we have made in job opportunities and childcare facilities since the 1960s. (The recent campaign against the Alton Bill on abortion and Clause 28 of the Local Government Bill are examples of the massive diversion of our energies). But this collection of essays is supposed to be a personal look at our own lives, to examine how we have accommodated motherhood in our practice as feminists: in this context, I cannot but examine my own weaknesses. How else can I retain the impetus for change and progress? So why have children? This was another question I had only half-addressed around the time I had decided on having children, and not on a very rational level. It is such a major decision in anyone's life and yet it seems to be taken almost automatically. So strong is the conditioning around this issue, that it is viewed as a phase in every woman's life, like puberty and old age. I had no great surge of overwhelming emotion for a cute, gurgling, bundle of joy that I assume women feel when they say they are feeling 'broody' (a horrible word which makes me think they are contemplating at least six children).

For me, the decisive factors were leftovers from my pre-feminist period and co-existed uncomfortably with my politics. I had a notion (unexamined) of the total loneliness of old age, and the only solution to this was children. My own reality stood in total contradiction. I was an only child and there was my dearly beloved father living out his lonely life in Delhi while here I was, in London, too far to be of any practical comfort to him. Still it was a powerful driving force. The other reason was my desire to replace my relationship with my father through my children. I had experienced the loss of my mother a few years earlier and constantly relived the imagined loss of my father. No other relationship had been as passionate and ultimately as irrevocable (after the upheavals of adolescence). Friends and lovers can be claimed as such only while the relationship lasts, then they become ex-friends and ex-lovers. But whoever's heard of ex-parents? So children were to represent a fixed point, a point of return, an immutable relationship in a world of flux. And, then, there was the other standard reason — an insurance against personal failure. If by any chance, I should fail to achieve the goals I had set myself, I would have the potential to live through my children. But the poignant contradiction in this position, especially for women, that women often fail to achieve their potential *because* they have children, was to return to haunt me later, after my son was born.

Through older friends of mine, I got the distinct impression that women who had had children in the early 1970s had felt alienated by the feminism, then current, which had rejected motherhood out of hand. Although radical

97

demands for twenty-four-hour nurseries showed a recognition of and sympathy for the difficulties of motherhood, the prevailing ethos appeared to rule out motherhood as an option because of the absence of a supportive social structure. Interestingly, for many middle-class white women motherhood had proved to be a radicalising experience. These women had experienced the personal fulfilment of motherhood, but because that unquantifiable, intangible experience soon vanished under the pressures of sole responsibility for the child, they threw the baby out with the bathwater. It was only when women continued having babies that the position was reviewed and motherhood was reconsidered, but in radically redefined family structures. Co-parenting, especially among lesbian women, offered a way out, although that path too was littered with its own problems. Communal living was another possibility. But when the experiment failed, the biological mother was often left holding the baby. On the whole, however, heterosexual women were largely caught up in the bind of the typical nuclear family.

For some Asian feminists, the extended family network provided a release from the pressures of solitary motherhood. For this and other reasons (such as the importance of the support structure provided by the family when living with the racist pressures of white society), Black feminists had reservations in concurring with the analysis of white women, that the family was a totally oppressive institution. The need to retain that support led Asian women into yet another contradiction. Most of us would agree that marriage only marks us out as the property of men and is, therefore, totally redundant and irrelevant to feminists. Yet, the majority of Asian feminists who live in heterosexual relationships have undergone the ritual of the wedding ceremony and/or registration to avoid family pressure and ostracisation. The guilt around this issue has made it yet another taboo area, rarely discussed and accommodated within our understanding of feminism.

It is seen as revisionism, as a cop-out and, so, surrounded by silence.

In the process of reaffirming the worth and value of women, feminists also reinstated the mother. Given the statistics of men who abuse their daughters, it becomes a heresy to talk of your love for your father. This also affects expectations around the gender of the child to come. To want anything but a daughter is a heresy in feminist circles. To be happy with either sex, which was my position, was to be too uncommitted. But these were just some of the thoughts and preconceptions that plagued me during pregnancy, and not quite as rationally as they have been laid out here. The uneasy fit as it seemed to me between motherhood and feminism meant that subconsciously I just compartmentalised motherhood as something separate from my political work. None of this was to prepare me for what lay in wait.

Disability. I had expected a short-lived contract of motherhood – five years of intense sacrifice, and then a clawing back of time lost. This was not to be. The delay in delivering my son left him severely handicapped. What stretched before me was a lifetime of commitment, more than I was prepared to give. The knowledge that my future was tied to this fretful, crying baby was painful and suffocating. Yet, when I was with him, watching him devour my time, resentfully, I found it hard to let go. All the political values that I had wanted to assert through child-rearing had to be shelved. I was working for such a basic level of development and self-sufficiency that I could hardly think about sensitising my son to socialist and non-patriarchal values. Nor, for example, could I think of developing a positive identity and culture for him as a Black person, when we would have to work for some years for communication of basic needs such as hunger, pain, joy.

Although we were, eventually, to start proceedings against the hospital where he was born, I felt, at a deeply emotional and non-rational level, that I had messed up his birth, and that I owed it to him to give birth to him again, to deliver him from his body as much as possible through physiotherapy and educational input. I was saved from falling prey to this myth of the tragic Greek heroine by my feminist views which located the source of his problems in inadequate healthcare. However, because his potential was essentially unknowable, I teetered from one extreme to the other – believing that my input was worth it because I was moulding a capable adult out of this bundle of spasticity and spasms, and at other times, wondering whether I should sacrifice my independence tinkering away at someone who may never achieve independence. This tension, this dynamic, when it worked well was healthy, and when it didn't it became a confusing and depressing see-saw.

At the time when my son was born, the effects of the Ethiopian famine were being flashed on world TV screens. There he was languishing in intensive care, hovering between life and death, sustained by the most advanced technology, every minute of life probably costing hundreds of pounds. On television, pictures of Ethiopian children dying, because undernourishment had left women's breasts dry and unyielding, mocked and taunted my concern for 6lbs of human flesh which I had yet to learn to love. Put that in the context of how the Third World is underdeveloped to maintain the West and you can see the personal benefits to be gained from living in the West. I, as a Black woman, discriminated though I might be by this society could not claim a complete sisterhood with Third World women.

It was the disproportionate time, energy and money spent on an individual that went against all my political views. My father's political activism (which had meant that my mother supported the family financially) had impressed upon me an ideal to which I aspired so that while most people watch out for their own, only few have the courage to battle against a system which destroys the chances of millions of people, at the expense of their own family. Later, I was to use a feminist critique to chip away at my father's heroism. He had done it at the expense of my mother's future. However, the central point remained – do I sacrifice my political work for one individual? – a consideration that hung over a tiny, struggling mass, clutching on to me, his lifeline, in a way that few mothers of able-bodied children experience.

And because he was handicapped I could not even use child-minders or state childcare facilities because that would have meant foregoing any physiotherapy that was available – leaving him to become a bean-bag child, left to stare at the ceiling. State provision for handicapped children is so appalling that women, if they can afford to survive on one income, their partner's income, are squeezed back into the house. In the case of single women and working women, State benefits do not even begin to cover the needs of handicapped children. Without skilled or adequate physio-therapy, a child with severe cerebral palsy can never hope to break out of her/his prison, the body. Although class, race and gender affect the development potential of all children, the differential effect of these forces is most obvious and painful with disabled children.

Within the constraints of economic reality, I tried to ensure that my partner took on a fair share of childcare. Emotionally, his presence was a source of strength, a rallying point. But in physical terms, I was left with the biggest burden. Although a handicapped child is accepted at a nursery from the age of two, and in respite care from the very beginning, these services are not widely available and the quality of care is such that I could not feel comfortable about accepting these on a long-term basis. The caring professions are so badly paid that all respite care I have used has had a succession of staff, a situation in which it becomes almost impossible to train each of them to look after my son for what turned out to be a few sessions only. Feeding and handling in the correct way was so crucial and so difficult, that very often he didn't get fed, or he came home stiff and unhappy.

Voluntary services, which included the Crossroads scheme, where carers were sent to your home for baby-sitting services worked out much better. Usually the same person was sent so training was easier. But the hours provided were limited giving me just enough time to relax. I was allocated six hours a week, two hours a day for three days, enough to find a quiet spot to regroup my dispersed energies and continue. It was not quite the atmosphere in which one could get down to writing or even reading. It was not just a question of practicalities. There was also the whole question of emotional trauma. Friends still ask how long I took to come to terms with it. But there is no such finiteness. Even today I am coming to terms with it. It is only as a young child's life unfolds that you begin to see the full extent of his/her limitations. Thank God, it doesn't hit you all at once. When you are told as the mother of a three-month-old baby, that the baby has suffered (in the jargon of today) an insult to his brain at birth, that he will be developmentally delayed, you don't think it means that he will never walk. You think it means he will sit at the age of eighteen months instead of six months. But today, when he is three and a half years old and still has the functions of a new-born baby, I am grateful if someone says that he might sit independently by the age of eight. Today, I could make such a prognosis with steel in my voice, but when he was three months old I could not have contemplated such a bleak future.

After a year, I decided that I needed to work part time for my own sanity, if nothing else. As respite care arrangements did not work out, I spent most of my earnings on childcare at home. Again, this was a decision I found difficult to make because employing another woman to share my childcare went against my feminist principles. At this stage, he was receiving physiotherapy five times a week at a centre which specialised in the treatment of children with cerebral palsy. I

102

had been incredibly lucky. The hospital at which he was born appeared to have a special relationship with the centre and their referrals were hardly ever turned down. Most children, especially outside London, had to make do with once-weekly treatment at their local hospital or an even rarer domiciliary visit, where the quality of treatment left much to be desired. One of the ways in which I coped with the emotional trauma was that I consumed vast tracts of literature about the condition. Intensive therapy before the age of two was supposed to be extremely beneficial and I came under the influence of an American form of physio-therapy which recommended nine hours a day, with the help of two volunteers per hourly session. I knew I couldn't cope with nine hours so I found a watered down English equivalent which suggested that three hours a day would be adequate. I gave up work and launched into this pro-gramme in my son's second year.

Finding thirty volunteers, and keeping them, built a sense of community which I had never experienced in London before. The stereotype with which I had come here, that you may bump into the same person at the local tube station daily without ever starting up a conversation, had remained intact. I had never felt part of a neighbourhood until then. We made some good and reliable friends. Many of the volunteers were sixth formers from local schools, one of the best hunting grounds for volunteers. Others were student nurses, pensioners and single women. Although I had expected mainly lonely, unemployed people to volun-teer, I was surprised by the number of people who had extremely busy lives and who were quite happy to take on yet another commitment. Thirty people, predominantly women and young girls, trooped through the house every week giving me little time or opportunity to feel isolated. With tea breaks between every session, the three hours quickly turned into five, and what with the mornings taken up with therapy at the centre, I had little time to myself. I spent weekends writing articles and fiction. Although the presence of the volunteers lightened the load, the routine was slowly beginning to grind down on me. The therapy was not working and after a year we gave it up. Even the jokes and laughter that had sustained us during that time took on a nightmarish quality in retrospect.

The parents I met at the centre where I had taken my son in the mornings, since he was four months old, provided yet another network of support. We set up a group to carry out fund-raising for the centre, and to meet the needs of the parents in other ways. The group was totally white and their concerns very Eurocentric. It was probably the only time that I felt the need for joining up with other Black parents. They were afraid of the word 'political' and refused to see that their intervention in the status quo was a political act. I found it quite difficult to operate in a group like this. Having said that, it was less racist than a lot of self-help groups can be. The interesting thing about the process of having a disabled child is that it breaks down preconceptions about the norm. Women having to face the prejudices of society about disability become far more sympathetic to other 'deviations' from the norm – Black people, single parents, etc. It might be also the first time that they have to grapple with the inhumanity and inadequacy of State resources, and criticism about living in high-spending Labour boroughs also begin to diminish. In other words, it is a mildly politicising experience. Perhaps it was this aspect that made me feel less alienated than I might have felt in such an environment.

Considering the number of support networks I had tapped into, I did not myself feel the need to meet other Black women in relation to disability. However, I was very conscious of the lack of provision, especially for those with language difficulties. I knew I had managed to secure many of the services by being assertive and wanted to set up a group for Black women caring for the disabled, a hope which I have yet to translate into practice.

As a socialist feminist, as a Black woman, I had no set

104

ideas of the 'norm' which were upset by the birth of a disabled child. I felt no revulsion in the presence of disability. In fact, I had a solid framework for critically analysing the way in which the norm operated to exclude anything which threatened the conservative impulse of the status quo. That did not, of course, mean that I was totally immune to the way in which the culture of normality and super heroes is flaunted – like visiting the local health centre where a mother proudly puts down her eight-month-old child who walks confidently across the room as the mother informs all and sundry of the child's age, while I lower my two-year-old son to be weighed on the baby scales because he cannot sit or stand on the scales designed for his age group.

Feminism also provided a perspective which lessened my sense of misfortune and 'chest beating' (an Indianism, meaning to feel sorry for yourself). It also enabled me to put pressure on my partner to take on as much domestic responsibility as possible. It meant I could go out for evening meetings and weekend work without feeling guilty, whereas many of the women who attended the centre spoilt the pleasure of their occasional evenings out by being weighed down with the guilt of making their partners do the baby-sitting. I understood the class factors that made it easier for me to cope – I had fewer financial worries and I was not ultimately at the mercy of the State. It also made it doubly important to campaign to improve services for the disabled.

Most of the women I worked with on various political projects hardly ever discussed childcare with me. Only those women who became friends, or those who had had children before, showed any interest in this area of my life. Most of the feminists I seemed to know were women who had children many years ago, or single lesbian women. Who looked after my child while I was at meetings was only my concern. Leaving early from meetings, or social occasions, always made me feel that I had failed to rearrange my domestic set-up to allow greater freedom of movement. I think that heterosexual feminists living within a nuclear family will be obliged to make compromises until such great social changes are brought about that childcare can become more of an undiluted pleasure because the State will have taken the stress out of it.

It is a particular transitionary phase of feminism through which we are living. Almost every ideological perspective striving for change sets up values and ideals which are impossible for all its adherents to follow and not merely because of individual weakness. Before that system changes, individual resources will dictate the level of compromise one makes with that system. Motherhood is almost, by definition, the Achilles heel of feminism. I hope this is not too complacent an analysis. As long as these contradictions do not take us backwards, but maintain the dynamic for change because we place them in the correct perspective, then such compromises will not be damaging to the cause.

Writing this essay has in itself been one step towards clarity, towards accommodating motherhood within my understanding of feminism. As I said earlier, I had a tendency to compartmentalise my life because it seemed the only way out. It is only gradually in the process of living with such a devastating disability that I am making the various bits of my life cohere.

Elizabeth Peretz

Very Much Part of the Experiment

February 1988. I'm forty this year, mother and provider for two children aged nine and eleven; research assistant, child development teacher, and doctoral student writing about the history of mothers and children. I have deep roots in the present in my home, and with friends and interests in Oxford, where I live. I also have strong ties with the past, with relatives and old established friendships. My mesh of anchors and safety lines reach securely over time and space, from the present back into the 1950s of my childhood, and from England over friends in two continents.

By the mid-1970s I was drawn irresistibly to motherhood, just as years before I'd been drawn to sex, and long before that to books and learning. I had a long dry thirst for these things as they appeared possible in the real world I lived in then. This new thirst I surrounded by proscriptions, plans, logic and precepts; but nothing would avert or assuage that thirst, I felt, but motherhood itself. I had strong ideals about bringing up children, from my profession, my political views, and my own childhood. These ideals have been only imperfectly realised for a number of reasons. I'd thought it possible to leave behind the media images of the family which left the woman, the child, and the man so trapped in separate disadvantages. The man an onlooker, the child powerless, and the woman a servant. Immersed in parenthood, I found these attitudes, which I wanted to avoid, springing inside me – attitudes already well established in people around me. I came face to face, for the first time, with many of my own weaknesses and my own anger, because I was finally in a situation which I felt unable to walk out of; children were inescapable responsibilities. I experienced very strong feelings with the children – and their father – joy, contentment, fulfilment – and frustration. My determination to continue a professional life and a personal life, as well as enjoy my children, has brought its own satisfactions and tensions. The equal parenthood I aimed for then seems more likely now to be achieved living apart than together; I have adopted far more of the traditional mothering role than I'd expected to; I have a longer record of failure in relations with myself, my husband and my children than I am comfortable with; but in spite of all this, time with my children, as a mother, is the most precious time I have, and the relationship I have with them brings me consistently the most joy.

In the beginning, I wasn't to be put off by friends who thought motherhood, like marriage, was a deep-laid trap which, once entered, would snap shut overhead with no chance of escape. I was confident of my own ability to change, to cope, not to be like the others, or more particularly, not to be like the mothers of the previous generation. I scorned the safe compromise offered by fellow feminists, to become a single mother. This seemed a real trap, a real disaster, from what I could see of the harassed friends in this position, alone with a small baby. My instinct suggested that my children would stand more of a chance with two parents at hand in a calm and secure home, so I worked towards such a model, hoping to create it without the traditional trappings and roles. But I left the belief itself largely unexplored. It is only experience that has taught me the minefields that lie underneath this calm image, and how difficult reinventing family life really is.

I embarked on a quest for a father for my children with all the determination of a 1950s women's magazine heroine. I knew very well what I didn't want; images of the cosy layette, the devoted but unfulfilled wife, the work-obsessed absent husband and father. I was much less clear about how the various contradictory ideas about my own future and my desired children's future would, in practice, work out.

So fixated was I on the abstract notion of marriage and motherhood that, aged twenty-three, fresh from the years at college, even planning a career was almost more of a preliminary move towards motherhood than an end in itself. I remember arguing, in a friend's bedsitting room, that a teaching career would be most compatible with childcare, and would, moreover, leave me free to follow a husband anywhere and still find a job. I taught child development in a further education college for three years, expounding the then fashionable doctrines on childcare and substitute mothering to young women who chose to work in children's homes.

In the courses I took at college and those I taught in this first job I absorbed many contradictory ideas about 'mothering' from the disciplines of psychology and social work, which I synthesised for teaching purposes, cobbling together classes for sixteen-year-olds from sheltered family backgrounds. Most of the research I was trying to simplify had been done either in laboratories, with babies and toddlers, introduced as experimental subjects or with children who had 'problems', or at least had been referred to professional psychologists or social workers on account of their 'problems'.

It was helpful, in the absence of the children themselves, to consider what theorists had to say. But once the children themselves had to be confronted, and worked with, in children's homes or special schools, it was obvious the theories were only partially relevant; it became more immediately pressing to deal with getting children up in the morning, coping with squabbles, getting rooms tidy, faces washed, and food eaten, however 'disturbed' they were. Knowing how to assess a child's conceptual grasp, or their point of language acquisition, had limited relevance, as did discussion on the effects of long stays in hospital. What the students really needed was to learn about the everyday tasks of being a parent, but these tasks were largely ignored as obvious or irrelevant by the course, and myself. The most successful students in practice were those who had been taught about looking after children from experience with younger siblings and years of baby-sitting, not the ones who excelled in class essays on theory.

The fashion in upbringing, then, was for child-centredness, in which the mother's role was to create a rich environment for free and optimal growth to produce free and near-perfect children. This paralleled ideas current in education where the teacher was to facilitate learning in the children rather than imposing it on them. The mother, at least with children under five years old, was assumed by professionals in health and social work to be the best person to look after her children. Professional advice to keep mothers at home with their children has been fairly constant for three generations. But the attitude to the children themselves has changed over this period. The professional's view of upbringing in the 1920s and 1930s entailed curbing, drilling, and maintaining physical health; at that time only a small number of people, mainly psychologists, were concerned with child-centredness. The research current in the 1970s when I started teaching saw the untouched child as perfect and self-motivated. No longer were adults to teach children; children were seen to have more innate wisdom than their parents. I learnt, and then taught, about substitute mothering in the years when Blake's *Songs of Innocence* were in vogue, and Truffaut made his films in praise of childhood. In this view of childhood, the rages and disturbances of early years were no longer seen as signs of savagery to curb and civilise. The mother, or other caring adult, was expected to see such rages as proof of a flaw in the environment and their own upbringing technique – punishment for their own bad handling. Habit training sank into the background; it was even assumed that if development proceeded correctly, a child would achieve socialisation, including perfect manners and cleanliness, unaided.

The mothering I aspired to was one of watchful guidance within a calm routine, with an equal partner who would share all tasks. My precepts of motherhood were all of cherishing, observing, and creating an environment for play. I saw ahead of me not a menial activity but an intellectually stimulating and highly responsible one which would still leave time for my own professional work in the adult world. My hours off would be covered by a day nursery, or preferably by the sharing other parent, father of the children.

Despite teaching about babyhood, infancy and childhood, and writing about it, I had had little personal experience of children. I had no younger brothers and sisters, and no close friends with young children. I was better acquainted with the children studied by Jean Piaget and Susan Isaacs, both of whom had written in detail of their observations of children at play; the strong emotions of these children were safely held away from me in the pages of a book.

111

The prospective father I had found while teaching these notions of childcare seemed suitable because he came from none of the conflicting worlds I inhabited at the time. He did not come from the middle-class, mildly cultured business background of my own childhood, nor did he spring from the socialist and intellectual world of which I was a part. The former offered men who would expect their wives to stop working; the latter, men who were intent on not marrying. Andy was an artist who took no part in the political debates I was steeped in. He had no strong opinions about gender and housework, gender and childcare, gender and salary. His presence was unthreatening; he represented an exciting new world of creating paintings which I admired and learnt much from. He was simply not particularly interested in housework, children, or whether I worked or not, provided he could paint; and I respected that, and was touched that he took seriously my desires for children, home, and some kind of independence.

Two years later, after keeping Andy and myself on my salary as I taught and he painted, I took my place amongst all those professional, highly qualified people who leave a good job in the hope of becoming a mother. I wanted, overwhelmingly, to be pregnant, bring up children, and have my own family. I continued to struggle for years with part-time professional work and full-time child-rearing which left the usual scars of chronic fatigue, and a diverse 'spotted dick' of a curriculum vitae. I can still feel the fear of childless spinsterhood that gripped me at twenty-seven, and the internal pressure to hold on to a relationship that promised children and shared parenting. I had enormous optimism about the future. I was certain I knew who I was, that I would stick to my professional work and become full-time again, before long, and that children, a partner and a home would make me finally happy for life.

I looked forward to having a family, with children and a secure home that I would contribute to from my earnings at part-time jobs, probably teaching English, child development, and marking exam scripts. Andy, husband, and the father of my children was apparently poised to take an equal share in everything. He also finally had a little part-time teaching, otherwise, in theory, he was at home painting and sharing housekeeping and childhood duties. Andy was strong, tall, and very loving. We were both happy to be at home, and seemed to have little need for money. We talked of looking after each other, sharing the paid work as well as the housework and childcare. After painting, the family was genuinely the centre of Andy's life, and I expected a similar pattern in myself. As part of the security, I wanted to be married, not because of moral imperatives, but as a joint commitment to a future family. I hadn't expected marriage to make an external difference to me, and was rather overwhelmed by the degree of acceptance it brought me with older wives and mothers.

Soon I had conceived. The months of pregnancy and the first days of motherhood offered all I had hoped. I'd been sold on the current 1970s dream of living 'naturally'. I consequently rented an allotment to grow vegetables, and bought as few trappings from Mothercare as I could manage. This last was partly necessity, since part-time teaching was not a well paid pastime. Nappies were boiled, marmalade made, and the baby, Jack, slept while I taught. It was hugely rewarding. Having a baby, much more than getting married, reconnected present and past, older relatives and newer friends who wrote, visited, and approved. I didn't want to leave the intimate nursery world for more than the two hours it took to teach a class, and was always eager to oblige when Jack cried for attention, and was delighted to so easily bring contentment by holding or feeding him. The world of college receded; life was centred on Jack and the immediate neighbourhood. I made friends with other mothers with tiny babies, and felt much better supported than they with Andy, my husband, painting at home while theirs left at 7 a.m. to return past bedtime. Soon — rather

113

sooner than expected, but much desired – we had a second child, Ruth.

The rewards of mothering were immediate and lasting. I have established a relaxed physical intimacy with both my children which tolerates anger and laughter, built up over a decade of washing them, reading to them, and tumbling about with them. The relationship I have with my children is the single most important part of my present life. The following diary entry from the year when the children were one and three years old, and no day was long enough to satisfy all our various needs, shows the strength of the fulfilment I had already found through their presence.

21 March 1980: Today I've felt very satisfied with the children and have, in fact, through the last 2 or 3 days. Jack is finally feeling happy in the social world – saying who his friends are . . . today he has cleaned the fire, done the washing, and spent all afternoon helping to make a fairly professional doll's house with me. The kind of thing I love doing – making it out of scraps, improvising; being with Andy has taught me to be more thorough, measuring, gluing, and pinning. How pleasing the next years will be with the house, friends, children, allotment, and Andy for support.

25 March 1980: Ruth's speaking is now very fluent, 'Would you want to come with me to see my house? I'se a robin redbreast,' and so on. Sense of colour – acute – sense of pattern and puzzle – almost as good as Jack's is now. Sentimentality – 'Are you my darling beautiful girl mummy,' and 'I'se sad and grumpy I want my mother.' Today Jack went to a friend straight from nursery for lunch and the afternoon, and came back a beaming boy of delight – what joy to be with.

But there were other aspects that have brought conflict

114

and depression. I would move from contentment, fulfil-ment, even elation to deep anger and despair within a week – sometimes within a few hours. Some of the reasons for this were within me; I found far more to respond to in Freud and other psychoanalytic writing after having chil-dren than I had before. But other reasons were external.

First, doing everything 'naturally' was extremely hard work, and so was doing with little money. Boiling and wringing a bucket of nappies daily, growing, picking, wash-ing and cooking vegetables, kneading dough for bread and running a food co-op for cheap fruit and flour, doing everything by bicycle or on foot because there was no money for cars or even bus or train fares – this, on top of breast feeding on demand, day and night, and being atten-tive to all Jack's other needs, was draining. I wanted to do this – I found it exhilarating and profoundly satisfying – but each day felt like a conveyor belt I never quite kept pace with, never had in control.

In addition to the fatigue came the creeping knowledge that I was not the detached observer in the laboratory nursery I had expected to be, but was very much part of the experiment. I was exposed to a raw and continuous emotional experience which included joy and pain. Rages and crying fits, I discovered, were part of even the most carefully guarded babyhood, and this childish emotion was exhausting, bewildering, and often contagious. The first night that Jack cried inconsolably, when he was several weeks old, was a revelation to me. I had tried every possible comfort, and these had been rejected one after another. The howls only increased, as I sat defeated in the dark, outside Jack's room.

I also found that my particular baby seemed to need help and companionship while he played, from me; he was not content left with toys alone, like the infants in the books, in fact, he seemed to have little idea what to do with them. He soon complained if I turned to get on with the household tasks, which seemed to have become gargantuan, and never

115

cooed contentedly while I read the paper, as babies were supposed to.

The equal parent I had counted on did not emerge. Andy had been out of the initial glowing limelight of mother and baby, and had established a quiet background role in his studio, from which he emerged only when asked. In the same way that I had, all too comfortably, settled into the primary mothering role, he slipped into the back-up housekeeping and caring role, without taking on the more usual male and financial parts of that job. As the months wore on, I minded this more. I began to need to escape, or at least to share some of the tasks, to rejoin the adult world for longer than a two hours' teaching span, and to lean on an understanding companion. I was extremely resentful when I found this all had to be requested; it was not freely offered, and much was not available at all.

Outside the pleasures of sitting holding the children, reading to them, or taking them for walks, and the continued satisfaction of teaching human development to student social workers, the reality of everyday life was of a battle that raged and receded, would be fleetingly won only to be rejoined hours later; the battle was with nappies, housecleaning, child washing, money and emotion. Journal entries from these years come the nearest to giving a sense of the gloomier side of this life lived on the edge; the following entries are from June and July 1980, when Jack and Ruth were three and a half and one and a half, and I was in part-time work, ten hours a week, spread over five short sessions at the neighbouring further education college. These episodes occurred only months after the more positive ones recorded earlier.

Sunday, 15 June. 10.30 p.m. I've been working cleaning the house since 8 p.m. . . it feels like a waste of an evening; I could have been writing, or planning courses; or sleeping so tomorrow would be better. But it needed doing, and I get some satisfaction from seeing it done. In fact, it would have been a fairly pleasant evening had I not had the memory of Andy's fury this morning. I lay weak and attacked by some throat infection and faintness this morning, with Ruth crawling on me while Andy stamped around downstairs shouting at Jack, complaining that the house was a squalid mess, a total muddle – it makes my temper rise to think of it. He says, laughing, that reason shows him to be in the wrong, but that he feels that its my job and follows his feeling not his logic – which includes shouting at me for this misdemeanour as he puts it. It's the kind of interchange that makes me go back over the last months to see what I've been putting up with. For instance; we hire someone to do the cleaning and a little baby-sitting. The latter is more appealing to Andy than the former – so less hours on cleaning, more on going out. Andy then decides its all too expensive, and says I should tell the person so. He insists all she does is clean floors and he'll do that. Goes and buys a mop and bucket. For two weeks, after much reminding, he does it. Since then – nothing. And the hoovering he was going to do? Once. I took over because the reminding or reproaching wasn't worth the candle. Tried to convince myself everything was fine – he was looking after the children and doing cooking anyway – as well as gardening and the house. But that wears thin now; two hours gardening in the last month compared to my stints; looks after children only when I work or do things connected with work – groans so much at these times that for their sake I don't dare ask another time.

The extremely practical, busy life of parenting at home was bound to be depressing for me. Reports of untidiness had dogged my school life and adolescent years. I had long ago convinced myself that I was not a practical person. I had learnt early on to aim at more intellectual pursuits. I found these 'practical' jobs difficult. I recorded in my journal that three hours floor washing, which I had just finished, could have been paid for with forty minutes teaching; and that for me floor washing was much the more taxing activity. Organising cupboards and washing floors was something I had never done, and had only watched other people do in modern well-equipped houses with adequate incomes. I was on an inadequate and insecure income in an ill-equipped home. Initially, this offered a challenge – rather like camping. But, following the mountain of washing which accumulates with a baby through from the dirty linen stage to the end point of neatly arranged drawers, with little hot water, no washing machine and no airing cupboard, was a huge task, and its accomplishment offered few external rewards.

Although I knew that at some time the shifting pattern of part-time work would be exchanged for a more secure full-time income I felt confident I would finally have, I had no desire to change my life radically. I loved spending time with the children, particularly outside where they could remain absorbed for hours in scrambling and climbing, or getting muddy, while I enjoyed both watching and joining them. On days of winter bad temper inside the house, I would rush to put on the children's leggings and boots, find the pram or pushchair, and just get out of the front door to sure and instant relief. Although, with Andy, there were the surface problems of sharing out home tasks, and the more fundamental problems of having few common interests, I loved spending quiet evenings with him, reading, being drawn, or discussing ourselves, other people, or the children. I needed to be held by him, looked after, when the children were in pain, or when I was ill. There was usually affection and warmth between us.

If different parenting models had surrounded us we might have sorted out a more sensible division of labour. Andy might have taken a more active part in the intimate and rewarding parts of the parent/child relationship which I guarded so jealously, and he also might have taken on some of the more arduous sides of housework; and I might have done more decorating. But Andy had no other artist-father to compare housekeeping notes with, and I had no part-time working mother. Through accident of class and place, the group of friends we belonged to presented a more traditional model of earning father, absent in the day, and home-bound mother. Parts of this model were changing; fathers, when at home, cooked, changed nappies, and took a full part in childcare; they stayed at home some evenings while their wives went to classes or had jobs. Their own fathers would not have done this. But they still pursued careers outside home which brought in the money to keep their wives and families. In retrospect, none of the families were as near to the media image of 'family' as I suspected them of being. It was more that I needed them to conform to a calm and comfortable image, so that when I called on them for coffee, children in hand, after a morning of tussles over eating and dressing at home, I could feel secure. And I liked that life, being like my own mother, visiting friends, concentrating on the children when the man had gone out, just as I liked the feeling of going out to work and having a purposeful role outside home.

We had other discomforts. Outside the immediate sphere of the neighbourhood, in the world of officials and professionals, our family fitted awkwardly into the prescribed social categories. Professionals with whom I came into contact – health visitors, doctors, and social security officials – seemed trapped in their own rigid definitions of family life. From time to time I claimed unemployment pay, and the following journal entry records one such visit:

Unsettled again with this morning's visit to the unemployment and DHSS offices. I take a certain pride in being odd, the mother who isn't single and yet draws dole. But I'm made uncomfortable by the assumptions they make about me and the family that I then have to refute by some clear statement – making myself the breadwinner with a househusband – I can see the next question in their eyes — why is the child with you then, and not at home with your husband? And why don't you have a full-time job? The unemployment people said they'd watch my application for money for dependents 'with interest' but had little hope; the DHSS said they wouldn't consider my claim at all if my husband was living with me. Where's the Equal Opportunities Board now?

I knew I wanted to take on full-time work again at some point, but I put if off; after school, childcare seemed too difficult to sort out, no suitable jobs presented themselves and I stopped looking for them, and life was so busy as I added committee work and volunteer work to my days that there was little time for more. Very few people I met made me feel I should be either a full-time mother or in full-time paid employment. An elderly relative or neighbour might let it discreetly be known they were sorry I had to work; once a Chilean woman expressed surprise that my education and career experience should be wasted at home. Ruth was on my knee at the time and Jack playing with bricks on the floor, a three-year-old full of interruptions. I found neither opinion convincing; I was entirely taken up with making the complicated pattern of days work. The day's timetable was extremely involved. In my neighbourhood, it was possible to have two-hours-a-day playgroup for the two and a half to three and a half year olds, two and a half hours for the three to five year olds, and a day that ended at 3 p.m. or 3.30 p.m. for the four and a half year olds and above. Institutions were not in the same street, nor were the hours of starting and finishing the same. Two hours a day would be spent pushing prams or pushchairs with tired children from one of these places to the other. My teaching, one- or two-hour blocks scattered through the week which, like the schooling pattern, changed from year to year, further complicated the picture.

It was not until I took on a salaried, full-time post that I began to understand what a fragmented and complicated timetable I had been following. It was extraordinary then to be in a polite adult world all day long, with several hours at a stretch in the same place, with my own books, thoughts and writing. It was a calm and protected atmosphere, in marked contrast to the taut and pressurised existence I had followed before. I've had the research job for three years now, but I might still have been negotiating part-time hours and outside interests if the job hadn't been directly in my path, making it impossible for me not to apply. As each hour to myself had opened up, when the children spent more time at school, I had filled it, and had more recently started to work on a doctorate. There seemed little time to take on more, although we needed the security and would welcome the money. This job allowed me to do research and earn money.

It should have worked for all of us. Andy never wanted to work anywhere but in his studio at home, painting, and my salary would free him to do more than that. The children could be with their father after school and then have me, refreshed and fulfilled, for the ends of the days and weekends. We'd finally have money for housework, clothes, holidays. At first, the arrangement seemed successful, but soon there was a creeping acknowledgement that despite the order of the home, despite my fulfilment at work, despite Andy's good-natured desire for it all to work, there was a gaping hole at home. Some evenings when I returned, exhausted from work, we would sit down to supper expecting a benign mother to walk through the door and comfort us all. I became self-absorbed, my centre in the adult world outside the family. I was surrounded at work by other working mothers, and supported in sympathy and by example in this new role. Andy was not so fortunate. School gate chat and child swapping in the afternoon takes place between mothers, not fathers who tend to be isolated and eyed curiously. The affection in the family remained, but the distance between Andy and me increased as I filled my head with the history of mothers and infants.

The sense that we lacked a family core increased despite a move to a new home, and despite spending weekends together. The more hollow we were, the more polite we became, until, finally, the taut atmosphere broke as Andy started a new relationship, I stormed with fury, and he left home. That was a year ago.

Being a single mother, centre of the family, I can hardly imagine a space for another equally involved parent living here. I feel as if, for myself, I have filled up the cracks, and that the three of us are growing, together, in a way that we never did as four. The same seems true of Andy and the children, in the two or three times they spend together in the week. We are now balanced, apart, in just the way I had longed to be, together. Although we both seem to need different relationships and a different life now, I'm still pleased to have had those intense early years together. I thought, in the beginning, I could turn myself inside out for an idea, and that whoever I shared parenting with would think so to. I imagined that two of us together could disregard those attitudes we wanted to avoid in our town or village, doctor or mother. I didn't know there were values too deep to pull out, nor did I know how many contradictory beliefs lived under my own skin.

Gillian Darley

Joseph

I want to describe a memory of motherhood. My baby lived not quite eleven weeks; he died, not slowly or even predictably, but between one hour and the next. But I do not want to write about that, of private grief or emotions too intimate to sit stark on the page. This is an account of motherhood glimpsed; motherhood as a finite matter which now, eleven months after his birth, eight after his death (odd how I find myself swapping those anniversaries around, depending on my state of mind) has a clarity and a completeness that may amplify other mothers' experiences by its very brevity and intensity.

I did it all late and untidily – as so many of us do. The option of having a child was drifting by. I had left it to chance, but that chance had not come up. I suppose the whole business was slipping out of grasp, an outcome arrived at by default. Always a godmother, never a mother, I muttered to myself in darker moments.

Then, in my late thirties, I became pregnant by a man I had all but broken up with, after an on/off saga of around three years, which had foundered on the rock of religious difficulties. I had never considered having a child without a father. I don't remember feeling whether the pregnancy answered any needs within me – the maelstrom outside was too confusing – but I found it desperately hard to decide on action. Eventually, I booked myself for an abortion. A woman friend with three children (the last of whom had almost died in his first week of life) broke the decorum that my confidantes had observed and pleaded with me not to do it. Then the father, too, intervened. I cancelled and spent a giddy fortnight telling everyone the glad tidings and sending more distant friends and relations the news tucked into my Christmas cards. Then, on Christmas Eve, after a bleak and frightening two days, I had a miscarriage. I spent New Year writing another heap of letters to put the record straight.

Now I was intent on becoming pregnant. This time, after a couple of months of blank depression, I became pregnant easily and it was entirely welcome news. What were a few personal difficulties in the face of having a baby? There were hiccups; something looking like rubella, a first amniocentesis which didn't 'take'; but Joseph arrived, naturally, and unblemished. Pregnancy had suited me, I enjoyed giving birth, but nothing prepared me for the reality of the new baby. I was almost paralysed by the joy that shot through me as I looked through the plastic side of the hospital cot that morning, just a few hours later, and caught a glimpse from the bright little eyes which, wide open, were waiting to engage mine. I have never felt emotion like it. My friends had told me as much – that it's just impossible to put into words. It doesn't work for everyone, but I was transported.

It seems, from where I am now, a hallucinatory period. I have a very clear set of physical memories. All the senses are engaged in these early stages of mothering; touch and smell playing as important a part as sight and sound. That delicious involuntary gurgle (his, and his alone, I now discover, even though every other baby does something like it), the feel of his skin that makes it hard even now for me to touch another small child, the odd mixture of the unique and the generalised characteristics all came new to me. I expected none of it. Those sensations have all stayed vividly with me, reminders which outshine the superficial veracity of photographs.

New emotions, new energy which seemed to be a tranference of the baby's own incredible and instant vitality to me, spread into other areas of my life. As a freelance writer, with work coming in nicely, I felt optimistic that I was ideally placed to get back to my desk soon. Before long, a month or, at the most, six weeks later, I was doing odd pieces – reviews and so on. Since I had written the last line of a piece the day I went into labour, giving birth seemed hardly to have dented my routine. I took Joseph along to exhibitions and began to organise myself for forays to meetings and other commitments, and I felt that my life was shaping up to my entire satisfaction. I had never been happier; I was a relaxed mother, my (by now) husband was revelling in Joseph's arrival, it bound us together and blotted out all the hesitations that lay behind us, and yet I still felt I had contact with my professional, individual self.

Motherhood, and the quantum leap that it introduced in myself, had established equilibrium in my life. (Or so it seemed in that brief honeymoon.) Now nothing remains but questions. Am I clinging to an illusion? Have I falsified reality; working mother for a month? Was I subscribing, all those years, to a picture – woman fulfilled by motherhood? I don't think so; my own mother's rather ambiguous attitude to the role did not fill my early years with many illusions in this direction. There was no saccharine image of motherhood available to me as a child, and absolutely no pressure on me to produce grandchildren – the traditional role of grandmother did not interest her. She had not enjoyed her child of her first marriage and her enjoyment of me, fifteen years later, was strictly on her own terms. The generation before had a cast list from Victorian middle-class fiction, down to a cruel nanny, a chill mother and an emotional (frustrated?) father. The precedents were not promising. As one member of my family said, knowing my fears on these grounds and seeing me with Joseph, 'You've broken the pattern.' It was a compliment that I treasure.

My mother was a contradictory sort of person; full of emotion but desperately awkward about its physical expression, intelligent but self-defeated, dwelling in the past in preference to the present, and in some fear of the future. The frustrations which she must have felt were transferred to me; she fussed over me, and when I tried to plead for space, she would recount in pained tones how much I owed her. I hated the idea that motherhood involved accounting with credit and debit columns being totted up as the years passed. I wanted to find that love was debt-free. I always felt that my father's love (I was his only child) came without the book-keeping element, leaving me free to respond. Yet he died, suddenly, when I was twenty at a moment when my search for independence was allowing me to give him precious little of my time or overt affection. My mother then retreated into an almost professional widowhood, from which she never emerged, and which sealed her off, year by year, from human contact.

She had been well over forty when I was born. That much she had always counselled; don't rush into marriage or children, there's plenty of time. I'm glad of that. When Joseph died she was still alive, but her mind had long since wandered off into senile dementia. She had, by then, become as infantile as my own baby. Senility brought people around her once more – nurses, companions, doctors – while I became for her, during much of the time, her own mother. While Joseph lived this was gently disturbing, but after his death it was agonising. A few months later, she died, a death as orderly and timely as Joseph's was untimely and catastrophic. A circle was complete, but upside down and back to front. The beginning ended before the end began.

The journey through the misery has involved hard work in clinging to that illuminated passage in my life. It is a struggle to remember motherhood completely honestly from here, and not to deny the exhaustion, the moments of exasperation, the things that did threaten to dent the perfection of it all.

But, it is perhaps worthwhile, at least to those who question the enveloping nature of this relationship, to describe where I am now, that is, life after bearing a child, but without it. The black invasive memories of one traumatic afternoon lurk in unexpected corners and it is not easy to fend them off. Routine, or at least what passes for routine for a freelance writer, has played its part. After a bit, professional friends began to guide me back to work, tactfully and gently offering me articles to do if I could. I did, I creaked back into gear – of a sort. I would shuffle forward and then lose impetus entirely. I needed deadlines as never before, and holidays and breaks threw me completely off course.

What I underestimated, and still am confused by, were the deeper changes that took place as a result of motherhood. I am not where I was before – not in a single detail. I have learned to pride myself on new abilities, some I had never considered of value. I was blown wide open by motherhood and by the emotions that came with it. A baby in those early stages brooks no hesitation, no procrastination. I was entirely willing to answer the insistent demands, my time was his. I had no idea that I could love that well, nor that I would find the patience to cope with the unremitting nature of it all. Conversely, other abilities by which I had set great store, producing words on

127

time, selling an idea, keeping myself fired up, all of which I had come to take for granted, seem useful but little more than that. But the real changes are probably concerned with where I see myself in the world around me. I suppose I had taken on protective colouring, childless, and likely to remain so. I had rationalised away quite a lot of feelings for which I had no use, buried some half-notions and aspirations which weren't going to come in handy. Reminded at every turn by what I was missing, I banked a great deal on what I had gained; an archetypal 1980s life of professional freedom, an excellent deal in almost every respect.

A reorganised but coherent working life was part of what I had expected from motherhood. I knew that my self-esteem, forged largely by the previous twenty odd years of working life, would hinge on how I brought that experience into a smooth conjunction with the bringing up of a child or children. Those expectations were not tested, the subject has become academic, but I remain convinced that what I learned in that brief span of another person's life will affect my every action, thought and emotion for the rest of my life.

In the meantime I have to regenerate the other, earlier self who survived without this knowledge. The desperate need for another baby has skewed my life completely, and that clear, defined sense of my own purposeful existence (the freelancer's lifeline, after all, replacing the idea of being indispensable to others with that of being indispensable to oneself) has weakened. We moved house a month before Joseph's birth. The house was for our family, large and comfortable. Now it is a nonsense for the two of us; we rattle about and don't know what to do with it all. In a way it is an apt metaphor. I feel the same kind of void within myself, an oversized space, underoccupied.

I have, as it were, a loose wire that hangs live from the ceiling. There is but one way to reconnect the supply, to rekindle those emotions, and that is another child. I discover I want, desperately need, those obligations that before I had my baby I used to dread. Those car loads of infants, manacled to the back seat, off on holiday or en route for school used to suggest the end of intelligent, independent life. Those bleary faces of friends, sleepless with sick small children, used to flash before me as a useful corrective to any fleeting broody tendencies. Now they are beacons towards that messy, exasperating, uncompromising existence as a mother that I nearly achieved. I wonder at my own contrariness.

The obvious alarms which another baby will bring, the spectral fears, are elaborated in the absence of reality. Actually, I suspect that different dangers lie ahead. The careless pleasure will never return, and I fear that the preciousness of another baby will tempt me towards that overprotection of which I was once a victim. We will inevitably take with us into parenthood a terrible need as well as dangerous shades of 'what might have been'. I have had my firstborn, but motherhood second time around will not be the easier passage that second children and their parents often enjoy.

I have chosen to make my journey without professional help, in the form of analysis or therapy, but with all the self-awareness I can muster, and some of the most understanding companions for that journey that anyone could hope for. My husband has been alongside, every step of the way. But, for all that, it is a lonely place to be, literally and metaphorically.

Motherhood brings you into contact with those who have already been there and with others who have just arrived. Falling out of contact with the women I had met during our pregnancies was inevitable once our common experience could no longer be a shared one. They had moved on; I was frozen out at week eleven. Without a baby, how could they or I bear to meet as their babies, born within weeks of mine, were living proof of what, in

129

the absence of medical explanation, leaves Joseph a victim of some hellish, statistical quirk?

Inevitably, my experience of having a child, the fulfilment that I most unreservedly found in motherhood, lacks perspective, especially when measured against the norm. It had no continuation, scarcely any development. What are eleven weeks of life? Any habitual timescale disappears in such circumstances. Those weeks were long in the living, immeasurable in the remembering.

This essay may read as a somewhat solitary rumination. That is ironic, since it all began, this new venture of mine, in a spirit of communality, joining a group of women with expectations and lives not unlike my own, and it has ended in finding myself apart. Again, in my close personal circle, three friends had their first children in the nine months before Joseph was born. Even without meeting other women, there was a readymade circle – for those conversations which so engross the concerned, but are so tedious to the outsider. Motherhood, so much a part of my friends' lives, has been and gone for me.

The arrival of my baby intensified all the other areas and activities which made up my life at that point. His departure has sapped and diminished all those same things – even, I fear, my essential life raft, my writing. But, after all, I am still potentially a mother, as well as the person I thought I glimpsed as I began consolidation of my working and personal life. I have to work hard to summon up the memory of myself before these traumatic months and build upon that in a new light.

Yet I know that the effort I have to make, perhaps am already making, is to convert that experience of being a parent, a mother, along with the misery of the loss, into a greater awareness of myself as an individual. To touch the depth of misery that the loss of a child represents, is to touch new aspects of one's personality. The profundity of the unhappiness is not a dead end; it must point you onwards. Several people wrote about that, in letters after Joseph's death and I found it hard to grasp. I understand much better now. Even so, I have looked at myself periodically, from the exterior as it were, and have been unable to understand how or why I am still functioning. The strength that I found, just to keep going, could only be explained by what had gone before. In the absence of a religious faith, I looked for, and found, the source within the experience itself. It came from the intensity and exaltation of feeling that motherhood has given me, a reservoir to which I can constantly turn and which was Joseph's legacy to his parents.

Jean Radford

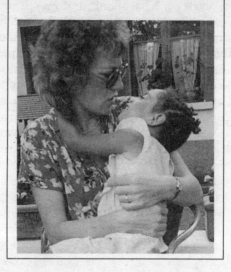

My Pride and Joy

Feminism, Julia Kristeva says, has produced a critique of traditional representations of motherhood, but has not yet produced a new understanding of women's continuing desire for children. I want to explore my experience of becoming and being an adoptive mother – a motherhood which does not begin with the physical processes of conception, pregnancy and giving birth – but which starts with the same desire – to have a child. My attempt to come to terms with that desire and to realise it with two children who were conceived and given birth to by other women drew me into a maze of fantasies and realities, onto ground which there's scarcely a language to describe. The practical, psychoanalytic and religious discourses on maternity exist, of course, and I make use of each in turn and in varying combinations. But Freud and Penelope Leach make odd bedfellows, and one of the problems of writing about motherhood is, for me, the language we have to understand it with.

So, here, I focus not on the daily grind and daily pleasures of being a mother, but on what it has meant to me, this desire for children, on how the experience of adopting has changed and continues to change its meaning. First, a flashback.

I was writing a thesis on Norman (no-man-maler) Mailer when I discovered feminism and my desire for a child and I was deeply resistant to both. Each pulled at the threads of my emancipated self. Motherhood was for other women, I was the clever daughter of my father and a puritanical Marxist for whom feminism was yet another diversion from the class struggle. These two positions were somehow woven together. Strangely, Mailer's contorted struggles with *his* male identifications unravelled my own. The melodramatic staging of his fears of femininity opened the curtains on mine, so that reading his books was like entering a theatre where the cast of characters was vaguely familiar. Caricatured, brutal, shocking, I could recognise not only the reactionary male politics targeted by Kate Millett but, dimly, my own positions and attitudes, my own divided lot. I was Rojack *and* Cherry, Sergius *and* Elena, Marilyn offering herself to a succession of photographers and Mailer running up the steps of the Pentagon to protest the war in Vietnam. As I worked through the American writer's shifting positions in the early 1970s, something shifted within me.

That's not right. Let me start again.

I remember one summer sitting in a garden in Leamington Spa. It is a neglected garden, unkempt, with long grass and trees but no flowers. I am telling a story about a botched operation and septicaemia, a brisk brave story with funny anecdotes till eventually I stop and fall silent, listening . . . *that* was the real beginning. When I was able to weep for the lost part of myself, for the baby, and for the body I'd deprived so effectively of its burden that it could never again betray me in that way.

In the next few years having dried my eyes (and finished

the thesis) I moved to London with the friend who'd listened to me in the garden and refused to laugh. My resistance to feminism had melted away and I threw myself energetically into the women's liberation movement. I did not talk about my desire for children in my women's group, but concentrated on other issues, the Working Women's Charter, the women's journal *Red Rag*, a local home-workers' group. There was a new identification with the women in my group, diffident at first, with painful moments of confrontation and difference and a new friend-ship with a woman – the first since my childhood – which remains with me today.

It was a time of excitement and activity with marches and demonstrations and meetings nearly every evening. But I remained silent about my wish for a child. That was the buried half of the equation, the secret bargain. If I struggled hard enough for other women, I might be allowed what I wanted, for wasn't I too a woman? Taking other women's hopes and fears seriously, I tried to do the same for my own. It was not self-indulgence or selfishness to wish for a baby but part of the larger struggle for women to get what they wanted and to create the conditions in which they might enjoy them. So why the secrecy? The personal was political I argued with the best of them, but it was difficult to voice the age-old desire for a child within the new political rhetoric. We want the moon and we want it now, I shouted in the streets, but at home quietly I began my own lunar calculations with thermometers and ovulation charts. Con-fiding only in the partner in my hopes, I waited each month, hoping against hope that I would conceive, that I would be given a second chance.

I waited in vain, and entered hospital for tubal surgery. The operation opened up one of the fallopian tubes, the purple dye showed that there was now a passage from ovary to uterus along which an egg could travel. In the weeks following the operation this opening closed. The tube was blocked, scarred, the purple dye got so far and no further. Guilt and despair set in. I would never have a child, I didn't deserve it. What I had spoiled and destroyed could never be repaired. I had denied my desire and turned away the most precious gift of all, and I was justly punished. A bad mother who had killed her child, I was rightly childless, forever damned.

Trapped in this melodramatic misery, like the princess in the tower, I spent years first trying to forget, then trying to remember and work through the sense of loss. I felt passionately about the Abortion Act and women's right to free and safe abortion. The personal and political matched perfectly here. I had lost my fertility and all hope of a child, but no other woman should have to. Meanwhile, there were other things to do, work, politics, friendships. I resigned myself to living childless.

The desire, however, was strong. It could not, would not, be blocked off – by scar tissue, medical opinion, or my attempts to deny its continuing existence. Like a subterranean river, it trickled into new channels. If I could not do it one way, there might be, must be others. 'I' would stop fighting 'it', and put my public skills in service of my private desires. 'We' would fight for a child together – *el pueblo unido jamas sera vencido*. What I wanted was a child, a relationship with a child. If I couldn't conceive and bear my own child, I would adopt one. Others had done this, why not I? I would apply to adopt a child and at the same time apply for further surgery. I would create my second chance.

The story so far. Too neat. Melodramatic. The romance of the drive, the ego combining with the id to overcome all obstacles. Is this another success story? Yes, and no.

In the next phase, the campaign phase, the obstacles are no longer within. I have to encounter the legal and medical worlds, only through these can I realise my hopes and get what I want. I read the medical debates on infertility, get out library books on human anatomy to study the structure of the body which I have ignored until now. I enter on a series of painful and unsuccessful operations in London hospitals, knowing that I must leave nothing untried, no stone unturned. I am now answerable to this driving wish for a child. Even if I fail, when I'm old I will be able to say that I tried everything.

I write in turn to each Adoption Society and to every London Borough which acts as an adoption agency. Months are spent in application letters and form filling. The replies are mostly discouraging: there are no children for adoption at present, our waiting lists for adopters are full. Or, we have toddlers but no infants, children with disabilities; and there are no white children. We write back carefully: we would like a child under one year, but we don't mind what kind of child, and we don't mind waiting. Only consider us. The Boroughs send us forms about our preferences, asking us to tick columns marked 'white', 'mixed race', 'black'. We tick all three. They write back asking why we want to adopt a non-white child. I try to explain that I just want a child.

The forms and interviews seem endless: our health, our family histories, the state of our relationship, finances, housing situation, motives are all up for scrutiny. I draft and re-draft statements about why I want a child, and this is the hardest area of all. There is a language for the social and material points, but the emotional and physical longing has to be rationalised or left out of the account. My desire for a child is subject to the Law – specifically here the 1975 Children Act and the social workers who act within its terms – but there are no terms to express the driving force which motivates me. In the language of everyday it's 'only natural' for a woman to want a child – the man wants a wife, the wife wants a child, the child wants a dog – but push beyond the nursery rhymes and the everyday assumptions about what's 'natural', what can be said?

On the forms and in interviews only so much can be said, the rest would be out of order. Completing these according to the demands of the legal and social work codes, I am forced to think about the unsaid, about my needs and desires. What is it I want? A child, a relationship with a child. But why? What is this powerful wish about?

A wish not to die without having experienced a close relationship with a child. A sense that whatever else I produce or contribute to the world – what I put into a book, for example – will in all probability not be important or of value in fifty years' time. What I put into a child will be walking the earth when I'm dead and gone. Something I've done will live on. I wish to adopt a child because I wish not to die? Absurd. It's about the future then?

But the desire for motherhood is also about the past. It's the desire to relive my childhood with the mother I desired to have rather than the mother I actually had. Is it that lost child or the lost mother I want to regain? Or both? To go back in fantasy, to recover, to make good, to change things for the better. Dear God, give me the courage to change the things I can change, the serenity to accept the things I cannot, and the wisdom to know the difference. The words of that prayer are the best words I could find, they give a shape and ritual to something in my wish for children. A child is a way of coming to terms with the past?

Back in the present: after two years of vetting we are approved as prospective adopters. Now it's a question of waiting and there is no guarantee we will be offered a child. During this period it's hard to hold the dream. There are no physical changes in my body to prepare me for the possible arrival, nothing but my desire, concentrated now into an image of myself one day feeding a baby of my own. So I get on with my life. I'm trying to get a full-time job, I canvass for the Labour Party during the elections, I write a review of Lacan's *Écrits* and look into the windows of Mothercare shops without going in.

Six months after starting a new job, there's a telephone call to say there is a four-month-old baby girl with an English mother and a Caribbean father, at present with a foster mother. Would we like to meet her? We visit the foster home with the adoption case worker who reminds us that this may not be the child for us and it's only an exploratory meeting.

She's brought into a room crowded with prams and drying nappies. Not much hair, toothless, a fat bald child in a scratchy pink dress. It is love at first sight. The cliché resounds in my head and I can hardly see straight. I feel as if I've been waiting all my life for this moment, for this child. I have. Magic.

We bring her home on 8 March 1980. A friend sends me a telegram 'CONGRATULATIONS ON INTERNATIONAL WINNINGS DAY' and I'm so happy I don't care if this is a loving pun or a GPO blunder. Even now, writing about it, the memory of that day silences me, it eludes description.

For the woman who gives birth, the arrival of the child must be a scene of separation, the end of a process as well as a beginning. She loses a part of herself, one becomes two, loss and gain. The once fused cell (ova-spermatozoa) has multiplied, split, differentiated into a complex organism which the mother expels, pushes out into the world to become a separate being, an other being. The physical separation, like other separations often accompanied by depression, is followed by separating out on other levels, for mother and child, over years.

For the adoptive mother the arrival of the child is a scene of different significance. The desire for the child is 'inside', but the adoptive child comes from 'outside'. Bringing the two together is more of a union than a separation and for me is accompanied by an almost manic joy. The 'I' who adopts this four-month-old baby is forced to recognise that, physically and symbolically, she is another being, formed by other bodies, in relationships I know knothing of. But in my imagination, she is the missing part of myself, at last returned. I am complete.

Impatient of intellectual and political distractions, I devote myself to my new-born love. There is gratitude, passion, absorption – above all gratitude – to the birth mother whose child I swear to love and cherish, to my own mother who gave me existence, to my newly found daughter who has given me this feeling. When I hold her, exhausted from the day's work and the disturbed nights, there is a deep relief and pleasure at finding myself able to give – again and again – what's needed: bottles, changes, attention. I've at last found the good mother within me, the ability to put someone else's needs before my own, and she's so beautiful it feels like a privilege.

In religious language, I am in a state of grace where petty anxieties and envies fall away. In psychoanalytic terms, I regress to a state of imaginary bliss, a narcissistic world where I am all-powerful, omnipotent. United with the one I love, as they say in popular romance, this is also the nearest I have come to Blake's lineaments of gratified desire. There is no one language to describe the experience. I sit in my own garden, now full of flowers, blossoming. I walk the streets with my pushchair. I hold the moon in my hands.

The story pauses here. I am reluctant to leave this brief golden age, this paradisal garden to remember the fall back into the quotidian. When or how did I return to 'reality'? To the reality of my limitations as a mother; the reality of my daughter's growing distance from me; the reality of other desires – the desire to work, to write, to take my place in the world again, not just as a mother, but in other ways. My beloved daughter is a part of me, but very different from me. She's optimistic, pleasure-loving, playful, whereas I'm fearful, serious, work-oriented. She's my other self, the one I did not become and I become stern or irritable at the differences between us, until now a source of wonder and celebration.

I begin to read articles by black social workers about white parents who adopt black children with a growing sadness. When she comes home from school and tells me the names she's been called by some white child, I say what I have to say, what I've often rehearsed in imagination. But although I say what a black parent might, I know it's not the same, not said from the same place. When I corn-row her tightly curled black hair, she says she wants hair like mine, thin, fair hair combed through in a moment. The day comes when she tells me she wishes she had a black mother like her and I'm hurt and proud at the same time. That night I dream I have a black lover and am pregnant. As my belly gets bigger my skin changes and I realise it's beginning to darken. In the morning I wake up white and flat-stomached. Neither of us can bridge that difference.

My fantasy, that if I love her enough nothing else matters, has to give way. I see that it matters to her, being black, to have two white parents and that I am not powerful enough in the real world, where black is different from white, to undo this. This is one of the things I cannot change.

My daughter came from a white mother and a black father. I can be a white mother to her but I cannot represent either that maleness or that blackness. I am after all incomplete, lacking. With all my love, I cannot be everything she wants and needs any more than I can shield her from pain, and that indeed I must add to her pain. What that means to her and will mean to her is her story. What it meant to me was the fall from omnipotence into a more chastened kind of love where I can only pray that though flawed and incomplete, I may still be good enough for her. Despite the arguments against trans-racial adoption, I can never regret having adopted her. How can I? She's my pride and joy, she gave me access to a realm I thought I'd never know, a love I'd never feel.

Meanwhile, she wants a baby brother, clamours for us to adopt another child, and specifies that it should be a boy. We want this too and apply again but without very much hope. The policy on trans-racial adoption has changed, our adoption society has pioneered the recruitment of black adopters and we are very low priority for reasons we acknowledge right. Then, too, we are almost too old, over forty. We wait again but more resignedly, and re-start projects put aside for our daughter.

When she is six years old, out of the blue comes another phone call from the adoption society. The mother of a three-month old boy up for adoption has picked our application forms out of the pile – as it were. It's the wrong time and the wrong place, since I have just accepted new responsibilities at work, my partner has re-started his book, and we have just moved into a smaller house. But it's another chance, another miracle, we feel chosen. We meet him and his mother, we say yes.

This time around it's very different. He takes the separation from his foster mother very badly, he cries incessantly and our loving threesome is totally disrupted. The next months are full of panic and exhaustion. My daughter suggests we send him back and it becomes clear that what she had in mind was a baby for herself not this demanding rival for our love and attention. My love for this second adopted child grows more slowly. Is this because he is the second child? Because of his temperament? Because he's a boy? I worry about my ability to love him as he deserves, but take comfort from the old sayings that friends and family offer: boys are more difficult than girls, two children are much more work than one, boys are slower, smellier, more clinging; or, he'll grow out of it, it will be all right, just do the best you can. During the bad times I cling to these clichés as if they were a lifeline, the only thing that will stop me from going under. This common-sense language of comforting half-truths is a net which holds me up over deep water. We draw closer to my own and my partner's families, whose love and support also help keep us afloat.

At work, times are also hard. Redundancy fears, increased workloads, endless paperwork and meetings as management administer further cuts. Colleagues are preoccupied, students need increasing support, and I can barely pull my weight. A working mother, I live not in the peaceful garden of my imaginings, but between two worlds, symbolically divided: the world of work which I experience as a man's world, where children are rarely mentioned; and the world of home, full of nappies, noise and perpetual mealtimes, where work still to be done has to be done after bedtime.

I lack the courage and energy to challenge this division and become, instead, a managing mother. I often feel guilty about leaving my adopted children to go to work, and drive up the A1 in tears after my small son has cried at parting. But I'm also proud of managing the ferrying to-and-fro, the child-minders, the job, the house and garden, amazed that I manage at all. Then, when I look in the mirror, I see a face haggard with lack of sleep, with frown lines on my forehead, and I grieve for my lost youthfulness. All gone. The constant fatigue has ruined my narcissistic belief in my eternal youth and strength. Sometimes I feel I ask too much, of myself, my partner and children, and that I give too little, to friends and to the world that needs changing more than ever now. I'm sobered by what I've taken on, and the child in me is frightened that it will all come tumbling down.

Now, my two-year-old son, with his small male body, strange and beautiful, is changing and growing. When I scold or smack him, his face crumples and the tears start. He turns to me – the angry impatient source of his misery – and holds out his arms to be cuddled and made better. The appeal is irresistible. His faith in me creates my faith in myself, he can ask and I can give. That to me is the miracle. It has taken me two children and some forty years to learn what other women, other people, seem to know from the beginning, or to learn in other ways. Perhaps this is what I most desired from motherhood, to stand here. This is my wisdom.

Stop here? or carry the story a bit further?

My growing love for the second child brings new problems. I watch my daughter struggling with her jealousy and remember my own passionate childish resentments. She is angry at his paler skin and feels betrayed by this and my new love for him, as she never was by my love for her father. I know she'll survive it, but am afraid she will turn

142

away from me, the unfaithful one. I will not let her give up on me. I vow that I will never give up on her, however rejecting she is to me. My desire concentrates here. If I can only hold on, I feel her life will be better than mine, she will at least not make the mistakes I made. I think with new sympathy of my own mother, how she too must have struggled with her jealous rejecting daughter, how she must have struggled to hold on. I have moved from being an envious daughter to being a grateful mother, as one day I hope my daughter will. But the daughter I was is still inside the mother I have become.

Feminism changed my conception of politics, has motherhood changed my conception of feminism? It has changed me, and my life. I rarely go to the meetings and conferences which once drew me like a pin to a magnet. Questions of power and identity which in the 1960s and 1970s were worked on at meetings, I now face at home.

Wanting a resolution I read through what I've written here. I see it's about childhood, language, working mothers, a love story with a difference, but says little that's specific to adoptive mothers. Was the focus on the desire for a child merely a desire to deny my difference from other mothers? To seek out what I have in common with, for example, most of the other contributors to this book? So that I could mingle and merge back into an imaginary unity yet again? Is it that there are fewer differences between natural and adoptive mothers than one might think, or that there are no words to express the difference? I don't know.

'You are not my real mother,' says my daughter to me. I did not feel either that my mother was my real mother, perhaps every daughter, every child, has this doubt. There is always the fantasy of another, more perfect, reality, of other possibilities reluctantly, if ever, relinquished. But what my daughter says to me is true, in a sense it was not for me. The gap between the ideal Mother, and the mother we actually have, is perhaps always there. If the Mother is the fixed perfect image of the ideal, a mother (small m) is always what falls short of that image. For me and my adoptive children, this gap between Mother/mother can be represented as the difference between the mother(s) who gave birth to them, and the mother who now looks after them. But if this way were not available, they would find other ways of representing the shortfall, as I did.

Anyway, I'm glad to have told this story, one day my adopted children will have their say, and perhaps their mothers too. I know I've only written one version, for there are a nest of possible stories here. Like the Russian doll I had as a child, one opens to reveal another, but the innermost dolly remains solid and unopenable, no matter how hard you scratch for an opening.

Jennifer Uglow

Medea
and Marmite Sandwiches

On the day I started to ponder how to write a straightfor-ward piece about what it was like having four children, two things happened. First I began to read *Beloved*, Toni Morri-son's strong, mythic novel which tells the story of Sethe, fleeing from the American South at the time of the Emanci-pation; how she swings an axe at her sons and cuts the throat of her infant daughter to save her from the slave catchers, and how the ghost of 'Beloved' returns to haunt her and her surviving daughter. It is based on a true story, of a mother with four children. In an interview the author talked of Sethe's act in personal terms, as the most extreme act of affection, and in political terms, as a symbolic refusal of the future subjugation of the Black race. But she saw it too as an assertion of self, 'our children are the best part of ourselves, they are our immortality, we cannot bear to think they will suffer as we have done'. Sethe could not have killed her child unless she thought she owned her. *Beloved* is not just about the chains of slavery, but about the iron bonds of motherhood and the terrible things it makes us do.

The second jolt came not from literature but life. My eleven-year-old daughter, brought up (I believed), on staunch feminist lines, suddenly declared over supper, 'You know, you are the perfect Mum: you clean, you cook, you love . . . and you look after us when we are ill.' I lapped up the praise, but I did rather quail at the terms. Leaving aside the facts that their father is far more domesticated, that I'm invariably in London when someone has to be rushed to casualty with Lego up their nose, and that the meal in question was cheese on toast and pears – why this stupendous fib? Did she think this litany was what I wanted to hear? Then I cracked it, 'Aha,' I thought, 'What does she *want*?'

What she wanted, it turned out, was to watch *Howards Way* on TV. I groaned, cajoled, protested; we watched it. And there, in a key scene, stood grandmother (round and comfortable) accusing business woman mother (designer chic), of neglecting her son (moody rebel); 'I know you have worked hard for your success, darling – but will you enjoy that success when you come home to your big house one night and find all the rooms *empty*?'

I began to feel dizzy. It seemed that while feminists are busy reclaiming a matriarchal legacy in everything from literature to science ('Mothers of the Novel', 'Mothers of Invention'), while artists like Toni Morrison find such resonance in maternal love, while psychologists unearth more evidence of our frightening power and anthropologists elucidate the role of the mother-goddess, most actual mothers are still trapped in familiar clichés – you cook, you clean, you love.

Questions flooded in. Those looming images, whether terrifying, like Medea, or piteously consoling like the Madonna, seem wildly remote from my daily life with its barrage of demands and negotiations ('For heaven's sake stop that noise! OK, but after *Neighbours* the television goes *off*! Have you cleaned your teeth/got your bus money/done your homework?'). After reading *Beloved* how could I presume to write on motherhood? My experience is padded by my place in history; I don't have to watch my children being dragged into slavery, hounded into ghettos, or dying in the deserts of Sudan. Even in contemporary Britain I am cushioned by accident and circumstance, not struggling on supplementary benefits or fighting racism on their behalf. Horrors may lie in store (my heart stops at the thought of a road accident, let alone a nuclear disaster), but isn't it too easy for comfortably-off women to lament about the juggling of roles as mothers, workers, individuals? Count your luck, girls. Yet on reflection I can see that questioning the problems of combining motherhood with the rest of our lives isn't just moaning. It is important because these difficulties afflict all mothers, whatever their class or income.

Another question which worried me was, why is it always mothers who carry the symbolic weight of care and caring? We cannot help but be moved by examples of maternal grief and anger – 'Las Madres of Playa Mayo', protesting for the 'disappeared' of Argentina, the Mothers' Committee fighting for justice for the murdered children of Atlanta, the photographs of mothers and children pinned on the wire at Greenham Common. But why, in all catastrophes, are the mothers always the first to be dragged out to weep in front of the tabloid photographers and the television cameras? Why not the fathers? Do they not feel equal pain?

Once you start thinking of motherhood in general terms you soon step into that treacherous terrain which Adrienne Rich describes in the foreword to *Of Woman Born*, as 'the most painful, incomprehensible and ambiguous I had ever travelled, a ground hedged by taboos, mined with false meanings'.

Because literature is one focus of my life (I work in publishing) it is there, rather than in psychoanalysis or sociology, that I look for understanding of 'the mother'. Yet if I practise a rapid sort of free association – within English writing alone – a very odd thing occurs. The images which rise up for me first are of mothers as dangerous, selfish, powerful; they almost all have sons; and they are invariably created by men, or by women who had no children.

Explain this how you will, but into my mind swims Grendel's mother, baying for vengeance on Beowulf. Then comes Shakespeare's Volumnia, drunk with vicarious power at the triumph of Coriolanus. From the novels of George Eliot, (so brilliant at depicting silly, doting, dependent mothers), step Mrs Transome in *Felix Holt*, hugging her wounds as her secret hopes of her son Harold are bitterly overturned, and Daniel Deronda's mother, the great opera singer Alcharisi. When Daniel was small she arranged for her son to be adopted by an English gentleman; both to free him from the burden of his Jewish past, and, even more, to free herself for her art. '"I don't mean to speak ill of myself,"' she tells him, '"but I had not much affection to give you. I did not want affection. I had been stifled with it. I wanted to live out the life that was in me, and not to be hampered with other lives."' Later she elaborates:

'People talk of their motives in a cut and dried way. Every woman is supposed to have the same set of motives, or else to be a monster. I am not a monster, but I have not felt exactly what other women feel – or say they feel, for fear of being thought unlike others. When you reproach me in your heart for sending you away from me, you mean that I ought to say I felt about you as other women say they feel about their children. I did *not* feel that. I was glad to be freed from you.'

Finally I think of Mrs Ramsay in *To the Lighthouse*. She now seems almost the most threatening of all, but how I longed for years to be like her, to sit at the head of a table, haloed in lamplight, dispensing *boeuf-en-daube* to an adoring tribe. Every time I rushed back to work at the end of maternity leave I promised myself that next time I would really take time off. I too would smile calmly, surrounded by my infants, knitting and offering consoling wisdom. It never happened of course. Mrs Ramsay remains a seductive image precisely because hers is the kind of maternal role the working mother has to learn to sacrifice. A necessary loss, but painful none the less.

Maybe all this implies that beneath the joys, I suspect and even fear my role as mother, while my blank about mothers and daughters points to the most mine-filled territory of all. Yet I confess that when I do turn to my own situation, the books which feel most relevant are not great works of literature but wry, comic accounts like Laurie Graham's *Parents' Survival Guide* ('the best things in life cost £23.99') or my second-hand paperback of Katharine Whitehorn's equally funny *How to Survive Children*. The coincidence of titles, several years apart, suggests an ongoing saga of middle-class evolution as seen through 'Woman's Hour' or the *Observer* – but if it's a case of the survival of the fittest then I imagine I'm doomed to go under soon.

The fact that I still have my head above water (just) is due to a wealth of life-rafts, (like work I love, good friends to moan to, escapist holidays and Mrs Swan who helps on Wednesday mornings), and most of all to my husband Steve. I keep thinking that his job as a law lecturer and all his work on deviance and authority ought to be helpful but (apart from reading *Noddy* for examples of police harassment, racism and community protest) in practice law seems to be as irrelevant as literature. So far we have survived four children: at the time of writing Tom is a serious twelve, undergoing the trauma of the first year at secondary school, enduring the slaughter of the innocents on the 604 bus; Hannah is eleven, fiery and loving, leaving the kitchen knee deep in flour in a whirlwind of cooking, exchanging mini-rugby for discos; Jamie is an unstoppable eight, besotted with wildlife and football, clad in the complete Chelsea strip, the only *possible* garb, even in winter, and Luke is five, prey to the inevitable addiction to dinosaurs, (fourth time round – I now know more about *Tyrannosaurus Rex* than the Natural History Museum). They all drive each other mad, with brief intervals of truce – like Christmas and birthdays.

I'm not sure that it is much more demanding having four rather than two (though I'm certain one is different). It's true that there are more odd socks, the ironing *never* gets done, the noise is more deafening and the house is permanently under siege by gangs of small friends with identical spiky haircuts and confusingly similar names. And with four the alliances and disputes are definitely more bewildering. The pair who swore never to speak again will be found within half an hour building an impenetrable camp in their bedroom with large notices warning the other two (whom you had just identified as their lifelong allies) to keep out on pain of a gruesome death.

But, while all this may not seem too dreadful to me, being one of four is often a cause for complaint among the children; they look with envy on the lot of the only child. More is left to them than in smaller families – in our house no one has a packed lunch for school unless they make it themselves (it's amazing what a spur a dislike of mushy peas can be). They also feel unfairly poor; the lucky members of their class who have fewer brothers and sisters always seem to have more, or better, presents. They would probably think that anyway but this assumption of poverty leads to alarming Thatcherite tendencies and a curious fascination with the stock market; they know they have to be millionaires if they are ever to achieve their aim of buying *everything* in the adverts. Time is shorter as well as money; you simply can't play chess, try to remember who Henry III was, do jigsaws and listen avidly to how beastly Mattie was to Alison, all at the same time. And I suppose it must sometimes seem as though love was spread thinner too. Though the mathematics of affection defy fractions, it does sound less convincing explaining that of course you love them most in all the world, but you also love a list of people as long as your arm.

I don't think we have ever worked out a parental division of labour, largely because it is easier to let things slide than to have serious discussions (read 'rows'). In fact, over the years, we have fallen into patterns based on time rather than tasks. I work in London for two days a week and stay overnight. These are his days: the other weekdays are mine; the weekends and evenings we share. This sometimes disrupts Steve's work: his time for research vanishes into child-collecting and trips to the dentist, while I despair when I get off the train at 8.30 p.m., still deluded that I am an independent career woman, to find a houseful of wash-ing. (How I hate clothes.) But on the whole the arrange-ment seems to work – it combines the dubious freedom of single parents (no need to refer or confer) with the equally dubious support of marriage – someone to explode at, laugh with and gloat to without feeling you are showing off. Having someone to worry with eases the load. For months Tom had a complicated knee injury. He thought it was quite a laugh being in plaster from thigh to ankle, but I was cast down by the fierce physiotherapy, the pain, the delays. It was to me, not Tom, that the nurses brought the cups of hot sweet tea. I wouldn't have liked to go through that, or anything like it, on my own.

The one real division of responsibility concerns sport. All our children, like their father, are sport addicts and my

151

complete physical ineptitude is the subject of ribald hilarity. Here I bow out completely: I don't even buy their boots and although I express the proper amazed delight at their prowess I'm a coward when it comes to shivering on the touch-line. This is less trivial than it sounds. Feminism has tended to underplay the importance of sport, labelling it as over-competitive, macho, aggressive. Yet we have to accept that it is fantastically powerful. Besides, the energy of children is overwhelming – if small boys have a spare moment they are wrestling or tumbling while girls are crashing down on the sofa with their feet in the air. Ours will play cricket or football until it's too dark to see and their interest extends beyond mere activity to a whole culture. My Saturdays are dogged by the need to buy football stickers (which are banned at school but still swapped fanatically in corners of the playground). I am glad that there is someone around who knows if Arsenal won the double in 1971 and can supply the names of obscure (to me) American football teams and women athletes. I used to feel left out, but now I've decided it's good practice to be totally peripheral to something central in their lives; maybe it will strengthen me for the time when they fall in love, or finally leave home.

Outside the shared family drama Steve and I lead quite separate lives – no bad thing, since this provides different brands of gossip and makes us impatient to be together. But, alas, this very closeness is a source of equal impatience to the children. We jealously guard our evenings, snatch weekends away, plan the year we will spend (alone) in Africa, South America, Indonesia. 'What, without *us*,' they gasp in unison, outraged at such betrayal.

The children know that we both work; his job is mysterious and takes place somewhere else, mine is all too familiar and mostly happens at home. Since we live in Canterbury, and full-time commuting would mean leaving at seven and returning at eight at night, when Tom was born I decided to give up my salaried job and to opt for freelance uncertainty. I have stuck to this because I want time with the children although it might seem more sensible (and tempting) to employ a nanny and return to a five-day week. Anyway, for all their lives I have worked from home, developing habits which now seem verging on masochism. The university day-nursery was a god-send which gave me odd mornings and afternoons, and later whole days when I started working in London again, but I still got used to snatching hours when babies were sleeping, toddlers playing with friends, children watching TV. There is no doubt that babies frustrate deadlines, disrupt timetables, fragment concentration. Infants are passionately jealous of books and blank paper, while a typewriter is an open invitation to bash and jam the keys. Then there is the telephone: as soon as they can talk they will insist on saying 'hello', (at length) to a harassed editor tapping her desk in a busy office. They are horribly clairvoyant and stage their disruptions with devilish skill. Once, while I was editing someone's book on the National Health Service a small child (deliberately?) climbed on a table and fell off, conveying clear signals of violence in the family. How did he *know* I was talking to a doctor?

Not only do children indulge in such subversion; they also wake you up early. This can be a bonus; although I think nostalgically of student days, when I slept till noon, now I often get up to work at 5.30 a.m. and have even persuaded myself that dawn is beautiful. I have also developed ferocious blocking mechanisms – useful on days when I have to type to a running accompaniment of the carpenter sawing, the radio blaring, children invading the study looking for lost toys, ominous yells and thumps on the stairs outside. Let them get on with it, I say. Not so useful when an idea hits while I'm standing glazed at the sink, toast burning, milk boiling over. But despite narrowed eyes and audible sighs they're very patient really, regarding this as a congenital weakness, like my total inability to catch a ball.

This year, for the first time in twelve years, we have no pre-school children. The new freedom ought to be total bliss – quiet house, long hours – but I find it rather unnerving. Indeed it was I, not Luke, who showed signs of severe separation anxiety. On his first day at school I had a vital meeting at work. Racked with guilt I rushed home from London, sure he would need me, arriving shaking in the playground just as he burst through the door. His face fell. 'Oh, *Mum*,' he wailed, 'Why are you here? I want to go home on the *bus*.' He did, I followed in the car, like the puny mother in a Heath cartoon, still dragged along by that monstrous baby, now of blazer-wearing size.

Because of the intersection of work and home, and the overlap of responsibility with Steve, I find it hard to sort out what is special to being a mother as opposed to being a parent. I do, however, take the point that even if the work is equal the guilt is probably not since fathers don't have to measure up to those awesome stereotypes of the all-caring provider and thus don't have to invest so much in details. One of my friends summed it up well; 'If *he* makes a meal and they don't eat it he doesn't feel rejected – he just feels plain cross.' To be honest, although I feel occasional stabs of guilt it doesn't colour my life. Perhaps it should (another thing to feel guilty about). Nor do I recognise in myself many other qualities traditional to mothers, least of all the much vaunted self-sacrifice and unselfishness. In fact, although you often have to put immediate desires aside when you have children, fundamentally, I see motherhood as a state of profound selfishness. 'Selfish' has such bad connotations, but I simply mean that motherhood involves choices and experiences in which women consider *themselves* in a variety of rich and complex, pleasurable and painful, ways – and we can easily forget this because we usually look outwards at the children and deduce that family demands diminish rather than strengthen the sense of self. Playing the part of 'mother' can even be a form of escape, an easy way out, an excuse for not achieving other goals. 'Motherhood' is a wonderful fall-back when anything else goes wrong – then I make it the centre of my life and say, 'What does it matter when I have the children: they are the most important things in my life.' This is true, but it is still a bolstering of self, not unselfishness.

There can, I think, be a kind of advantage in the way having children breaks up the linear flow of women's lives, and gives the sense of having different centres of self. If (and it is a big 'if') women are free from other constraints, such as poverty or lack of opportunity, such breaks encourage a curious awareness of flexibility and freedom from rigid career structures, a potential for choice. I have long felt this, especially as I meet so many women who have had one career, then moved on to others as their children grow, so I was intrigued to see it expressed from a man's point of view by Ian McEwan in *The Child in Time*. The novel's hero reflects that such mutability, such 'remaking yourself' is an aspect of femininity, an 'unruly' element arousing jealousy and hostility in men. At a certain age men freeze into their fates, while women know 'they might just as well be doing something else'. What appears a weakness could become a strength.

> Committed motherhood denied professional fulfilment. A professional life on men's terms eroded maternal care. Attempting both was to risk annihilation through fatigue. It was not so easy to persist when you could not believe that you were entirely the thing you did, when you thought you could find yourself, or find another part of yourself, expressed through some other endeavour. Consequently they were not taken in so easily by jobs and hierarchies, uniforms and medals. Against the faith men had in the institutions they and not women had shaped, women upheld some other principle of selfhood in which being surpassed doing.
>
> Ian McEwan, *The Child in Time*

What is the essence of Mrs Ramsay if it is not 'being' as

opposed to 'doing'? I would never underestimate 'doing'; it is vital for women to be free to achieve on equal terms with men. But while Mrs Ramsay is passive (though effectively so) if one remembers Virginia Woolf's rejection of 'hierarchies, uniforms and medals' in *Three Guineas* one can see that this choice of 'being' can also be active, even revolutionary. There may be a positive distinction for women to make about their lives, in choosing not to achieve in a worldly sense, but to support continuity, the circularity of existence.

In Britain today, although there are still struggles to be fought on contraception and abortion, motherhood is itself a selfish choice. We can (or should be able to) choose not to be mothers. The decision to have a child, if taken knowingly, is taken because of what we feel they will add to our lives, not as a generous gesture to the future of the human race. If free from complications, childbirth itself, although it *is* painful (*pace* Leboyer, Kitzinger et al) is an experience of such intensity that it seems to push one over barriers onto a different plane. If you avoid post-natal depression (there are plenty of 'ifs') then the early months, despite sleepless nights and sick on the shoulders, are full of pleasure in small things – a smile, a step, a word. The rewards continue later, the clinging arms, heavy sleepy limbs, the knowledge that you are the centre of someone's world. Yours is the name they cry in the night, the person they run to, perform for, kick when things go wrong.

Such emotional and physical awareness extends outwards into other areas of life. Simply being used to touching makes people more demonstrative and I find that I now consciously have to hold back from touching people I'm talking to or putting an arm round someone who looks low, because I'm so used to acting this way that I forget the 'proper' boundaries. This assumption of physical closeness within the family has its dangers. The revelations of child abuse make this clear, but the reaction of some people has been almost equally disconcerting – as if we shouldn't find out *more* but should keep the doors around the family tightly shut. Yet, surely control comes from awareness, not from suppression.

Emotionally, the constant exposure to that extreme openness of childhood with its the heights and depths of feeling, also seems to unlock jammed doors. New fathers, more than mothers, say they are taken aback by the way they respond more emotionally, not just to people, but to films, books, items on the news. This too has its darker side; all mothers I have spoken to have experienced moments of unreasoning rage over trivialities (the four-year old who refuses to get dressed), and have stamped off to kick the cooker instead of the child. For me, as with physical demonstrativeness, these newly released feelings tend to turn outwards. I feel more delighted, but also more aggressive on the children's behalf than I ever do on my own. It is difficult to hold back from fighting their battles for them, but that would be dangerous (and anyway they would die of embarrassment). You just hope that in the last resort they know you are on their side, against the world, let alone the teacher or the boy next door.

One 'selfish' gain of motherhood, which is less equivocal, is the way you see things through fresh eyes. There are rediscoveries as well as discoveries: animals, woods, the theatre, books. Memories flooded back when I watched Hannah last summer, lying on her stomach reading a battered copy of *Wuthering Heights*. Because she found it on the bookshelf of a holiday house it came unfettered by any label of 'literature' and she devoured it, as I first did, as passionately and uncritically as if it was *The Little House on The Prairie* or even *Dallas*, ('I *hate* Hindley, why is he so *beastly*? *Surely* Cathy can't marry Edgar? *Why* does she have to die? Oh, poor Heathcliff!'). I know too, that having children has galvanised my flagging political commitment. Pure protectiveness makes me care more about the future and as my eldest son and my daughter watch the news, ask questions about Ireland, worry over Chernobyl or express angry disbelief at apartheid, I relive the first confused outrage I felt when I started to think for myself.

There are other unexpected new perspectives. One major omission so far has been the difference having children has made in my relationship with my own mother, whose grandchildren have tapped strengths which I did not see before. She has trekked across Europe with us and camped in ridiculously small tents with an obvious enjoyment that defies notions of age, is appealed to on everything from wild-flowers and birds to politics and religion and her intrepid directness usually proves far more useful than my carefully qualified answers. Even more important is the way that my role as a mother has led her to talk about her own life, and mine, in a way which has prompted new respect and affection.

I have also become involved more deeply with my extended family, with Steve's parents, my brothers- and sisters-in-law, and their hordes of children. And more new vistas have come from outside the immediate family. This is a common experience, which mothers can't avoid even if they want to. Doors start to open the moment you are in the ante-natal clinic, whiling away the waiting in intimate conversations with women you would never otherwise meet, whose worlds are miles removed from your own. Whereas the intimate joys of having children are equally shared by men (and since they've been allowed into the delivery room they beat us all at blow-by-blow accounts of The Birth), these border-crossing conversations do seem mostly confined to women. This is partly to do with patterns of work — one only has to look at a school playground to count the fathers on the fingers of one hand. But the club of mothers, while immensely supportive, is not without its perils. For one thing people like me don't show up well there: ('Mum, you *will* come early and you *won't* wear that old sweater will you?'). Also competition seethes beneath the comradeship. You either play the game (if Class I are doing 'fruit' you should rush off to Sainsburys for a mango, not stuff an old Golden Delicious in his satchel) or you opt out with a sneaking feeling of disloyalty ('Oh he's hopeless/never could tie his shoelaces/absolutely hates maths').

But I enjoy all this really. I like the windows opening on to different lives, different worlds. I cannot make any claims for mystical maternal power but nor do I personally experience motherhood as oppression, though I can see why many women do and I certainly hold my head in defeat at times. I hate the detestable tea-cosy smugness which cloys round the word 'motherhood' when spoken in a certain tone. I deeply resent the notion that being a mother represents 'fulfilment', as if women without children were somehow incomplete. I fiercely object to philosophies of early bonding, or glorifications of childbirth, which imply that a woman who adopts or fosters is somehow less of a 'real mother'. I do not believe that motherhood is all; if a woman finds that she needs to leave her children to save herself, although there is bound to be shock and distress, it may be that she should get out as quickly and as painlessly as she can. It could never be an easy decision and once made, should command sympathy and support.

My own experience, though exhausting, though it sometimes seems a crazy way to live, has been a good one – so far. This seems truly more due to luck than judgement. As our children grow and change, and new pleasures, new battles, take the place of the early ones, I feel I live in a constant state of surprise and suspense. It is like reading the best of novels, combined with being in love; I want things to stand still yet can't wait to see what will happen next. And, above all, I don't want the story to end.

The Best of All Worlds?

From an early age I wanted to have children, love children, rear children. And later, teenage fantasies placed these children in a traditional family setting; I had a husband and home and was not a single parent, liberated or otherwise. Whether this feeling could be called an instinct and whether it is something linked to my sex and so a maternal instinct; or whether it is linked to my desire to perpetuate my genes and so a human instinct; or whether it is a cultural thing, learned from my environment and my desire to be like everyone else, I still do not know.

It certainly was there. But it was pre-dated by an equally strong determination, which had nothing to do with parenthood or motherhood – and that was to be 'something' when I grew up. And this something was in no way linked to my being female because I had no idea what sex I was during my first few years. First, being born during the war and not realising that any other condition existed other than that of being at war, I wanted to be an RAF pilot. Obviously, I was not aware that I was a girl. Later to my surprise the war ended and this ambition changed to wanting to be a doctor: we had a small baby in the house, in the shape of my sister, born when I was nearly five. I clearly remember the health visitor telling me that girls were generally nurses, not doctors – and my surprise at her statement. Not long afterwards, as a result of finding tremendous pleasure in books, I decided to be an author; but finally, actually became a journalist.

Yet, by my early teens I was obsessed with the idea of myself as the ideal mother. Career ambitions were on a back-burner and I spent happy hours working out names for the children, fixing a suitable career for my husband and designing the ideal family home.

I had also become aware that I had been born a second class citizen, an inferior member of the human race. This realisation slowly dawned in the same way that, years later, we gradually came to realise that our youngest daughter was burdened with something far more difficult for her to come to terms with and which also would not go away – her epilepsy.

Given a choice all those years ago I would have chosen to be male, but the dissatisfaction was only a vague one and, as I was a realistic child, I recognised the condition as inevitable and accepted it. Besides, it was pointed out to me that I would be able to be a mother, carry and give birth to children, something not permitted to the other sex; this was something hugely exciting and desirable to store away in the imagination for the future.

By the time I was eleven indoctrination was complete. I can remember my teacher at primary school saying, 'You could be the first woman prime minister, Margaret.' The name was right, but she had the wrong girl! I heard her words but rejected the idea completely, thinking it not possible, not worth striving for, not even worth considering. What feebleness! What a change from the pre-school person, unaware of sexual differences and looking forward to being grown up in a world where no such differences existed.

The conflict was arising, at the onset of puberty, between the competing needs of my bodily and mental development – and at this stage the needs of the body were winning hands down.

I knew I wanted to be a mother. My body pulled me in that direction and environmental influences pushed me that way just as strongly. My parents wanted secure happiness within a family for me. It was not that they said anything; but one just knew that was what they wanted. And few of my friends had mothers who had careers. It just did not happen. Proper mothers did not go out to work. They stayed at home and cared for their families. My father, a teacher, spoke vehemently about the horrors of 'latchkey children'. His boss, a man of tremendously strong personality, mesmerised me at dinner one evening by telling me that the best thing a girl could do was to provide succour for her husband in his career. I absorbed it all, unquestioning. Now, my own daughters, and sons too I hope, have learned to think differently – or at least to think for themselves.

Yet my parents were fervent believers in education. They were proud of me when I did well, annoyed when I slacked. But they believed in education as an end in itself, not as a means to an end – that end being a better position in society or a career. And though they talked about my future career there was always an unstated assumption that the career would take second place to motherhood.

That was the way things were in the 1950s. However, when both their daughters and their daughter-in-law decided in their own ways to have the best of both worlds they accepted that with parental pride and no words of criticism.

I was at a girls' grammar school where the largely all-women staff was also largely unmarried – failures, in our teenage minds. There was no way we were going to be like that. The fact that the war might have robbed these women of potential husbands never entered our hard little heads. We were going to be proper married ladies, with husbands. What was the point of studying too hard? It was more satisfying to give these women hell in class and outside class apply ourselves to finding boyfriends. We were not waiting to be swept off our feet, we were out and hunting – and this from a quite early age, say, about twelve or thirteen. We did not think of the boys as friends, or even much as people, but as possible husbands and providers, and we concentrated on developing characters that would appeal to these potential recruits – docility, prettiness and a willingness to put men first in the pecking order.

Looking back, I find it curious that we chose to rebel against our teachers rather than our parents. It can only be that, because our teachers were the only career women we came across, we equated a career with spinster status and, in the first flush of sexual development, rejected it.

Many of my friends achieved fairly steady relationships, lasting a year or even more; this was in many ways good, for they could then get on with concentrating on other things such as passing exams, or just developing as people. I was singularly unsuccessful, being noisy, unpretty and incapable of small talk with boys of my own age. I knew I had to conform, to become a less ebullient, more docile person if I was to succeed in doing what I now wanted, which was to become a wife and mother.

This character training took years of what I now consider to have been wasted effort. But in the meantime I needed something else to serve as a prop to my self-esteem – a career idea. I chose newspapers for no other reason than that I liked talking and writing and had become intoxicated with the sound and smell of the presses following a visit to the local newspaper offices. Newspapers meant Fleet Street at that time and the problem was how to achieve it before finding a husband who would provide the next stage of home and large family. Twenty-four, I decided, was the latest I could leave the wife and mother bit. I announced to my father that I wanted to be a reporter and would leave school at sixteen to do so. He recoiled as though I had said I was going on the streets. Actually, looking back, my plan was not so bad, but parental views can be very persuasive.

I went back to school work to achieve what they wanted, a place at university. I was not against the idea really, so I did not lose any sleep over it; merely put in the minimum effort to succeed. Spare time I filled with things that had no immediate link with sex, career or school work: hockey, swimming and reading.

In fact university was a wonderful experience – three glorious years of freedom, learning and indulgence. After a year, in the summer vacation, I met Geoff. You could say he was the best thing that happened to me. Loving him freed me to enjoy my studies and the multitude of other experiences university offered and freed me from worry about amorous relationships, or the lack of them. On the other hand, feminists could say I opted out; by choosing the security Geoff represented I rejected the chance to stand on my own two feet and to make myself into that 'something' I had wanted to be as a small person. Thinking about it, they could be right, though I prefer to believe I was keeping my options open, hoping to achieve a best of all worlds – a loving family and self-fulfilment through a career. Whatever the reasons, I found myself at the end of three years, a part-educated, inexperienced, married, trainee reporter. Real life was about to begin.

Geoff and I knew we wanted children and once we had

sufficient money to put a good deposit on a house we decided to take the plunge. Three children, Andrew, Patrick and Ellen, arrived in three years. We had no car, no television, no phone, no washing machine, no expensive holiday desires, and no wish to put the possession of them above the desire to have children. I was a reporter but gave up full-time work when Andrew arrived. The future stretched ahead and the career could wait. We could look far ahead (though it seemed like forever at the time) and foresee the days when I could return to work and we would be financially secure. That time has come and the years that have passed now seem to have disappeared in minutes. I do not regret the path we chose, though with a different background, or in a different decade we might have gone along a different route.

All my friends in North Devon either had babies or were busy having them and I eagerly joined the production line. I never found looking after the children either boring or a negation of myself as a person.

The women's movement was virtually unheard of in that neck of the woods and, in any case, I felt that the children needed my full-time attention during their early years and would get it. I was not being forced into anything I did not enjoy; and the bits of domesticity which I did not particularly like, such as cooking, cleaning and shopping, went with the job.

It is possible I might have felt differently if our children had not appeared so quickly and easily, and if I had had time to start moving up a career ladder before they arrived. Then, I might have rankled at the subsequent lack of personal freedom, and the fact that I had absolutely no money of my own. But only occasionally did this hit home: there was the day I bought a skirt and realised it was the first time for a year I had bought any clothes apart from knickers and tights; and the time I went for a walk completely alone and thought how pleasant solitude could be. But, generally, these things did not matter; we were

165

happily married and enjoyed the world as it was rather than grumbling about things we did not have.

Now, I find it odd that I was quite so contented because I was never really cut out to be a housewife, as distinct from mother. I neglected housework to do the things I enjoyed, such as playing with the children and taking them for walks, visiting friends, sewing, reading, playing hockey and squash and later, getting involved in local politics. I can only assume that if you get what you have always dreamed of, you are content, for a while at least. Mind you, three years of constant pregnancy and babycare will not leave even the most independent-minded female much time for thoughts of higher things.

We moved from Devon to Oxfordshire in 1967 – and that was a major change; an eye opener. People appeared much better off and far more sophisticated.

They lived in Cotswold stone cottages with exposed beams, ingle-nook fireplaces and antique furniture – or at least the people I wanted to be like, did. They had cars, phones and holidays abroad. And their homes were always tidy. The women did not go out to work, but glowed with self-assurance. I was envious, a feeling I had never had before. Away from the cocoon of my parents and old school-friends in North Devon, I felt I had lost my identity. I stopped being content with being a wife and mother.

The move also came at a time when the three children were less demanding of my constant attention so I had the opportunity to branch out. I started writing a weekly feature for the local paper, not so much for the money, but as a preparation for an eventual return to full-time journalism; and I joined the parish council and a number of committees. At the same time I rejected specifically women's interests, refusing to join either the WI or the women's movement. There was a lot of bloody-mindedness involved in those rejections: if I was going to make anything of myself away from the home and family, it was going to be as an individual and not as part of a women's group.

So when our youngest child, Emma, arrived, part of me was pulling strongly in the direction of career and self-assertion. I had seen the future and what it could hold, and wanted both that and another child.

When Emma was stricken with epilepsy I believed she was being punished for my selfishness in putting myself before my family. I have never been able to escape completely from the feeling that a woman's place is caring for her family, raising the next generation, keeping the home together and sublimating herself to her family's needs. Common sense and logic tells me there can be no link between Emma's disability and my partial abandonment of the traditional woman's role, but logic does not always have the upper hand, and I still search for things I might have done wrong when she was a baby, which could have caused the epilepsy. And I still feel guilty.

Emma's first fit happened when she was about eighteen months old. It was a febrile convulsion linked to a high temperature, and we soon forgot it. But epilepsy was finally confirmed one awful Christmas when she was three and a half. I have been waiting for it to go away ever since and release her from its burden, and us from the pain of seeing her suffer. If this seems melodramatic I am sorry, but life can be difficult enough for even the most fortunate, without the added cruelty of a disability. It just seems so bloody unfair on her!

I had first come across fits as a little girl of about six or seven; there was another little girl living in the same road who was epileptic. She did not go to our school and was rarely allowed out to play. We all knew that she was strange. She did come out one day and, under the big chestnut tree where we were all gathered, fell to the ground in a fit. Her father came, took her up in his arms, and carried her home. 'Is Julie all right?' I asked her mother. But her mother turned away and went home too, without replying.

I did not fully understand her reaction then, though I do

now. She had allowed her little daughter out to play with the rest of the awful, ordinary kids and the attempt at normality had failed. I never saw Julie again, because we moved to another house shortly afterwards, but I often think about her now.

The juvenile curiosity and sadness I felt on seeing that little girl lying in her father's arms bore no resemblance to the horror and panic I felt when my own children went into convulsions. For Emma was not the first. Andrew had two fits. The first time, I thought he was dead as he fell on the floor with a cry, shaking and turning grey. No amount of baby-book reading had prepared me for that and I ran crying up the road, holding him in my arms. It took the proverbial slap on the face from a retired doctor living nearby to bring me to my senses.

I went on reacting like that for years and have only slowly learned that I am powerless and can do nothing until the fit has spent itself.

We are brought up in these wonderful modern times to expect too much. All will be well in this best of all worlds. By and large we have little direct experience of death or suffering.

We are taught that if we love and care for our children, they will live happily ever after; antibiotics will cure their sicknesses and broken limbs can be quickly mended. In other words, when something goes wrong we expect to be able to take action to put it right.

But there are not necessarily going to be any magic answers with epilepsy, or for any disabled child. When Emma had a fit, my whole being screamed 'do something' but I could no nothing. I felt that week in, week out, I was being brought face to face with death; the death of the thing most precious to me in the whole world, my child. Night after night we would awaken at the slightest sound and rush into her room. Sometimes we would find her sleeping peacefully, sometimes shaking uncontrollably. Or occasionally during the day her actual silence would alert us to the fact that something was wrong and we would find her lying on the floor beside her bed. It was not that this happened all the time but that we could never relax. If we dared to say that Emma seemed well, or that she had not had a fit for, say, a week, or a fortnight, that would be the cue for an attack.

Panic, despair, helplessness, guilt, sadness at her lost opportunities, worry over her future, tiredness, hope – I shall never give up fighting for her – and above all, love: the emotions aroused by our youngest child can never be anything but powerful. They are, in fact, the same emotions one feels for any child, but greatly magnified in intensity. They are love made exhaustingly painful and without the promise for a secure future that modern mothers and fathers take for granted as justification and reward for their years of devotion.

But do not think that Emma was a burden. She was not – and is not. A disabled child can be a blessing in a family. Emma certainly is – a loving, tender, vivacious and friendly girl, who happens to have fits. She is the most open person I know: thinking about her brings tears to my eyes and whenever I set off in the car towards London to bring her home for the holidays I feel a tug of joy in the pit of my stomach. Loving Emma is like the perfect pearl of the fable – unblemished and true. I am grateful to her for it.

But this knowledge was far from me when she was born. As with Andrew, Patrick and Ellen, my first words when the effort of giving birth passed and I heard her cry were, 'Is she all right?' Mothers never expect the answer 'no'. It is something they dread and for which no one is prepared. I had read every baby book under the sun during my pregnancies. My first thought on waking was always, 'I'm pregnant; I am going to have a baby; it's there inside me, growing.' Those baby books all had paragraphs about handicaps; just a few words on convulsions and epilepsy. They sounded disastrous and I prayed they would never happen to my children – not, I am ashamed to say, for their sakes, but for mine. I thought I would not be able to handle it, would not be able to cope. We never had any illness in our family when I was a girl and it did not fit in with the dream concept of the perfect family. It is a hard lesson: even as I was teaching my own children that life was not always fair, I was having to learn that lesson for myself. And Emma, of course, has to live with that lesson for the rest of her life.

In fact, Emma's disability links our family with families in the past, with families in the Third World, and with the animal kingdom of which we all still form a part. Here, suffering and early death were and still are very real facts of life. Disability in the family has taught us all a powerful lesson: do not take life for granted. Has it made us better people? I do not know and, quite frankly, do not care. I do not want Emma's condition to have been good for my soul or for the souls of the rest of the family. If the others have learned love and understanding by being in contact with their sister, all well and good. But we would swap all that if she could only be well. I am not prepared to rationalise and say that it could be worse – though it undoubtedly could. I can live with it and I think she can too, but I wish she did not have to. I do not like the idea that good can come from her suffering. I do not want her to suffer. I do not want her to lighten the world like Jesus Christ or Little Nell. I would rather she were well.

Emma is now at a special school for children with epilepsy and soon takes up a place at a college for disabled students. But she did not go away from home till she was sixteen. Geoff, Ellen and I left her at the school one September afternoon and before going home went for a cup of tea in a nearby café. We sat there in a certain amount of wonder; a burden of worry had been lifted from us – tea in a restaurant can be a dodgy affair if one of the party is likely to have a fit and hurl the cups to the floor. Now, if she had a fit, there were others who would also care. The sense of relief was quite physical. Other people were actually happy to share the responsibility for Emma. And not only did they not think Geoff and I were neglecting our duties as parents by allowing her to go away from home, they believed it was right for Emma.

It had taken me all those years to come to terms with her illness and to realise she was a person in her own right who ought to have an independent existence. She had a right to be away from her parents and it was not a crime to let her go. But I did not think that at first. It took teachers and care assistants, less blinded by family duty than I was, to make it clear that Emma should go away to school. I know why I did not want her to go. I was being tugged in different directions by my own needs and what I felt were hers. I just could not decide on the correct course of action. Sending her away seemed like dereliction of duty.

One thing is certain; I had a real old guilt complex because deep down I felt a good mother would have abandoned all thoughts of a career and stayed at home. I know mothers who have done this, where mother and child have no other existence apart from their shared life. But I have, subsequently, met other mothers of children far more disabled than Emma who have clear-headedly decided that a life of total self-sacrifice is wrong for them, for their disabled child and for the other members of the family.

We took that decision, though at the time there was no one around to give us any moral backing. We just supported one another. Anyway we both believed that Emma's condition would get better as her brain matured, so, at five, off she went to school like Andrew, Patrick and Ellen had done. I would have a career, Emma would be cared for by us at home and we would take things as they came.

And it worked well; not perfectly, and sometimes it was a bit of a muddle; but it worked well. You cannot be a working mother unless you have support from somewhere: housekeeper, nanny, the extended family, husband or children themselves. In my case it was Geoff and, increasingly, the children, as they grew in maturity. Geoff not only fetched and carried and looked after the children in the school holidays but, most importantly, backed me in what I wanted to do. The regular tensions that arose when things did not run smoothly were nothing compared to the tremendous support he gave me and the pride and interest he took in my work. Unless husbands join in this partnership, a mother may be able to hold down a job but is unlikely to be able to turn it into a career.

The children learned to do things for themselves and to live in a less formal family atmosphere; and as a family we learned to be flexible – one person's needs would give way to another's, if both could not be satisfied. And if I could not be around to do what they wanted on one occasion, I would be there the next.

Looking back, my having a job involved a rather muddly kind of caring in which we played things very much by ear from day to day, term to term. At first I used to make them all a cooked breakfast before leaving for work. Later, they made their own and discovered toast and cereal. School dinner replaced my home cooking at mid-day. After school they came home together, did their homework and watched TV. They grew up as sensible, as resilient and as well behaved as I would have wanted. They learned to cook and to use the washing machine and the iron – though never to tidy their bedrooms. Geoff and I arranged days off carefully so that one or the other of us could generally cover if the other was away or if we were needed to take them on a special visit, or were needed to watch the latest nativity play or school concert. If the children suffered through anything it was through parents made edgy by concern over Emma.

In fact, Emma was not too bad during the early years, otherwise we would have had to get paid help in. With the benefit of hindsight some sort of help in the home would have been a good idea, but then, I had felt if I could not manage I should have stayed at home. That is one of the annoying things about motherhood – or life in general; you only learn the answers once you have been through the problems.

However, I did learn fairly quickly that it is impossible to run a full-time career and do all the things that a woman without full-time employment can do. Hockey went, so did the local parish council and the village newspaper. And with great fortitude I vowed never, for the foreseeable future, to join any committee or pressure group or even to be a member of anything.

As our children grew and started becoming far more independent, their relationship with us changed. We found we had four individuals, inhabiting four noisy bedrooms and demanding the right to their own thoughts and their own opinions. I find it quite funny to realise that though I brought them up to have minds of their own I still get irritated if they disagree with me. Where did these four individuals come from? Our genes are in them; our teaching is in them. But they are not us; they are other people. I can see bits of me and bits of Geoff in them all: love of sport, love of a good argument, high handedness, friendliness, untidiness, inertia, bossiness, and a certain intelligence. But where on earth have the other bits of their personalities come from?

Why is Ellen a vegetarian? We fed her the most succulent bits of the joint on Sundays, but they still ended up under her high chair. I know where her argumentativeness comes from – she and I are me and my own mother all over again. But where did she get the ability to charm complete strangers and light up a room when she comes in? And why is her bedroom, full of bits and pieces, a work of art? Where did Emma get the ability to give love so generously? I know why she is noisy, but where did she get her enthusiastic innocence? Why is Patrick so composed; so self-contained; so generally reasonable and so very pleasant? And why on earth is Andrew, the first on the scene, in a home with no money to spare, brought up

173

to share his possessions and for whom early life seemed to mean perpetual motion, now working in a finance company?

To our first three we have now acknowledged their freedom. Having a job away from the home made the transition easier for me because it taught me that I was a private person away from the home and they had to become private people too. But even so, anger and arguments would erupt as I tried to protect them from the difficulties and dangers that lay outside, and as they countered and sought to go the way they wanted.

And I found it sad losing the intense involvement I had had with them during their early years.

For me, one of the supreme delights of motherhood was the passionate intimacy I had with my small children. They could not hide anything from me – and did not want to. They came to me for everything and my life had an extra dimension through them. Later they became private people, and I had to learn to judge when to try and help and when to leave them alone. I remember one of them lying in a bedroom, suffering the pangs of love; there was nothing I could do to make it better.

I was no longer their only confidante; their friends learned their secrets before I did. Now I suppose they have secrets that I will never hear about or have any right to hear.

The change was gradual though and because we had four children we were able to enjoy one child's steps towards the future while knowing there was another still needing us completely. And of course, having a life away from home meant I was not totally tied to them for self-fulfilment. Even so I shed tears when both boys went off to university. I cleared their rooms of old socks, and lay on the bed and wept.

The years between complete dependence and independence were happy ones. Those special routines which all families treasure as their children grow, helping them learn, the ritual of the bedtime story, trips to the country-side, are something never to be forgotten. And if anything symbolises the ideal of family life it is those years before the children reach adolescence.

But those years are now a memory; boxes of holiday snaps and drawers full of school reports, exercise books and innocent school diaries. The person I loved as a pretty six-year-old is very different now he is twenty-five. He comes home for Sunday lunch, does his washing and tells *us* how to run our lives. He loves us, but he doesn't actually need us.

Mothers with grown-up families will all have their own views on how to raise children. There is no one right way, that is certain. I do not believe you should mould children to your will or try to break their spirits to achieve good behaviour or conformity. I don't think this attitude was a licence for our children to run wild, though. We made it clear what we believed in because we knew there were plenty of other people around with different ideas, only too willing to step in and fill any gaps. I have always tried to explain that other people have views which may be different to my own but which are perfectly acceptable. As long as they know the alternatives, and why different people think and behave as they do, I believe my grown-up children will be able to make sensible decisions.

All these problems that arose as the three eldest trod the bumpy road towards adulthood were magnified as we worried about Emma's progress. The perception that we must care for her is acute. We do not resent it. We might say, 'why did it happen to her?', but not 'why did it happen to us?' We cannot plan ahead with any confidence and we cannot see a time when we can do more or less what we please, which is something, surely, most reasonably happy married couples must look forward to. Any sort of planning is short-term, complicated and time consuming. Emma's free education runs out at nineteen. We want her to continue training, but how does she get it and what is available? Our next job is to sort out the complexities of adult training, allowances, places to train and possible jobs. What does a young disabled person do all day if she cannot find some sort of employment? We do not want to wrap her in cotton wool for the rest of her life, but we cannot say, 'You are eighteen; get on with life.'

I hope we have guided our older children towards fairly normal adult lives. Our next need is to allow Emma to develop as an adult too.

Julia Vellacott

Motherhood
in the Imagination

'If you have children, I hope they won't come in such a way as to spoil your shape the day after you're married; nothing is more vulgar than to be pregnant a month after the wedding . . . once you've been married two or three years, let governesses and tutors bring them up. Be the kind of lady who represents the home pleasures and splendours.'

Honoré de Balzac, *The Marriage Contract*, 1894

Women are the agents through whom men become either healthy or sickly; through whom they are useful in the world or become plagues on society.

William Buchan, *Domestic Medicine*, 1763

Think of the Sabine Women, their breasts exposed, who never left their children, not even on the field of battle. They gave birth to an exceptional race of men.

André-Théodore Broachard, *De l'Allaitement maternel*, 1867

'Sacrifice is a dated idea. A superstition, really, Mother, like burning widows in India. What society is aiming at now is the full development of the individual.'

Mary McCarthy, *The Group*, 1954

Psychical inacceptance of the maternal function and defective maternal function (are) . . . frequently related to the normal failure in women to establish the erotic function.

Marie Bonaparte, *Female Sexuality*, 1973

Loving a baby in this way is the best investment that there is. It pays dividends from the very beginning and it goes on paying them for all the years that there are . . . Fun for him is fun for you. Fun for you creates more for him and the more fun you all have the fewer will be your problems.

Penelope Leach, *Baby and Child*, 1977

There are many different ideas about what it means to be a mother, and endless prescriptions for 'success'. Advice and ideals shift constantly – the only thing that doesn't change is that women are prepared to listen. The reason we do so is our own longing for certainty. If we cannot find this certainty in ourselves, there is a powerful pull towards expert knowledge that will tell us how to be a good mother. For it is difficult to be a mother: it involves a lot of giving in a situation that often arouses our own most infantile feelings; it carries a burden of responsibility towards our children – the feeling that their well-being now and in the future is in our hands, though however hard we try, there always seems to be something that escapes us. In this chapter I want to look at whether the notion of a mother who can satisfy her child's longings is illusory, and to ask, if so, where does that leave us?

I will first look at what different experts have said about mothering and child-raising over the present century in order to make clear that we live not only with our own fantasies of motherhood but also in a climate of changing social norms. This is very difficult to sense when the meaning of motherhood is presented in such absolute, 'natural' terms. Later in the chapter I shall try to see whether there are theories of motherhood, or identity in general, that allow us to think more freely about the figure of mother, in a way which is analytic rather than prescriptive.

It is mothers who have been the greatest target of official expertise, since the beginning of the modern family in the mid-eighteenth century. Jacques Donzelot, in *The Policing of Families*, points out that while the family might help to reproduce the existing socio-economic order, it is in fact 'the systematic inability of families – some if not all – to perform the relevant functions which accounts for the interventions in the family – interventions which not only keep the families in line but also transform them and thus constitute them.'[1] By interventions he means not only psychological expertise on mothering, but also the many financial, judicial and educational pressures exerted on different family members to perform a range of social functions. Here I will look at attempts to regulate mothers through the imposition of authoritarian psychological norms – do this, and you will be a good mother.

A fascinating account of the attempts of experts to influence the lives of women in the West is given by Barbara Ehrenreich and Deirdre English in *For Her Own Good: 150 Years of the Experts' Advice to Women*.[2] Much of this advice concerns instructions for motherhood.

The aim of 'scientific' child-raising as expounded by experts at the start of the century was to prepare children for industrial life. The new behaviourists advised mothers to mould their children as early as possible into patterns of regularity, discipline and self-restraint – whether in feeding, bowel movements, sleeping, bathing, play. The one thing to avoid was any irrational overflowing of maternal tenderness. J. B. Watson, the early behaviourist, wrote in 1928:

> There is a sensible way of treating children. Treat them as though they were young adults. Dress them, bathe them with care and circumspection. Let your behaviour always be objective and kindly firm. Never hug and kiss them, never let them sit on your lap. If you must, kiss them once on the forehead when they say goodnight. Shake hands with them in the morning . . .[3]

However, with the rise, from the 1920s, of economies increasingly dependent on individual consumption, discipline and self-denial began to seem counter-productive and a new doctrine of self-gratification began to appear. Many mothers in the 1940s were still plugging on with the disciplinarian Truby King, but by the end of the decade psychoanalysts and other child experts were launching an attack on the notion of moulding a child into regulated behaviour. The task of the mother was now to follow the free play of the child's spontaneous development. A text on *Child Behaviour*, written in 1951, states:

> First of all, recognise your child's individuality for what it is and give up the notion that you either produce (except through inheritance) or that you can basically change it. Recognise it, understand it, accept it . . .[4]

One thing the child did require from its mother was her unquestioning love – 'To the childraising experts of the thirties and forties, to love is a mother's *job*.'[5] This love was not something reasoned and disciplined but deeply instinctual and libidinal – indeed, it was the mother's ability to regress to a childlike state that enabled her to establish such a close, necessary and fulfilling bond with her child. Naturally, all mothers would be supported by working husbands, and free to devote themselves full time to their children. In the late forties and fifties, 'the mass media poured out the same advice to women of all classes. Women who worked, no matter what the reasons, were depriving their children and denying their deepest instincts.'[6]

After a while, however, doubts about libidinal motherhood began to creep in. If, in this romantic union between mother and child, there were still children with problems, something must be wrong with mother. Indeed, just as mothering was guaranteed by a core of unconscious instinctive love, so mother's unconscious neuroses must be at the root of the 'psychotoxic' diseases of infancy – 'what really mattered now was not what the mother read or thought, what she wanted to do or tried to do, but what her unconscious motivations were. And instincts couldn't be faked.'[7]

'Motherhood as pathology' appeared in two main forms – the 'rejecting mother' or the 'overprotecting mother'. Or you could be both at once. Betty Friedan wrote:

> It was suddenly discovered that the mother could be blamed for almost everything. In every case history of the troubled child; alcoholic, suicidal, schizophrenic, psychopathic, neurotic adult; impotent, homosexual male; frigid, promiscuous female; ulcerous, asthmatic and otherwise disturbed American, could be found a mother. A frustrated, repressed, disturbed, martyred, never satisfied, unhappy woman. A demanding, nagging, shrewish wife. A rejecting, overprotecting, dominating mother.[8]

The next honeymoon to fade was that of the child. By the early 1950s there was already official doubt about what later came to be called 'permissiveness', and talk of the need for 'limits'. By the end of the 1960s this had become an openly anti-child, anti-youth mood. In their account, which is mainly American but which reflects feelings elsewhere in the West, Ehrenreich and English describe in detail the wider social events underlying this shift: the feeling, in the US, that 'Mom' had emasculated American manhood, as evidenced by the 'demoralisation' of troops in Korea; the news of hardworking, nice-mannered children in the Soviet Union, culminating in the shock triumph of East over West in the Soviet launching of Sputnik in 1957; the rise of youth protest movements in the 1960s which the experts tried to explain as a 'generation gap': 'Clearly American youth was unfit to face the Enemy. Then the movements of the sixties came along and revealed that youth *was* the enemy.'[9] After the shooting of four protesting students at Kent State in 1970 a national guardsman is said to have commented, 'I wish it had been forty!' From this it was a small step to the wave of films such as *Rosemary's Baby* in which children were allied in some way or other with the devil and the powers of darkness, i.e. subversion.

Meanwhile, there began to be an ever greater tension between the culture of self-gratification and the romantic ideal of female self-sacrifice. Where was mother in this rush to consumption? Faced with women's growing protest against feminine self-denial, the psychomedical experts began to find everywhere a 'rejection of femininity'.

> Among the conditions which the gynaecologists in the fifties and sixties began to view as psychogenic, or caused in one or another by 'incomplete feminisation', were: dysmenorrhea, excessive pain in labour, menstrual irregularity, pelvic pain, infertility, a tendency to miscarry or to deliver prematurely, excessive nausea in pregnancy, toxaemia of pregnancy, and complications of labour.[10]

This diagnosis showed the experts in retreat: 'Women simply would not flog themselves to live up to that masochistic ideal: they *were* rejecting their femininity.'[11] The initially personal revolt against imposed ideas of feminine identity and sexuality, which found such powerful expression in women's consciousness-raising groups, formed the early foundations of the women's liberation movement. But the gap left by the now-discredited psychomedical experts was hardly cold before a whole new generation of experts arose in the form of pop psychology. The new ideal was fervently anti-masochistic. The talk now was of 'realising human potential' and 'self-actualisation' — what matters is *you*. A flood of self-help paperbacks and therapy books gave instruction in how to be free, how to live in the here and now, have fun, put yourself first. Ehrenreich and English quote the 'Gestalt Prayer':

> I do my thing, and you do your thing.
> I am not in this world to live up to
>   your expectations
> And you are not in this world to live
>   up to mine.
> You are you and I am I, and if by chance
>   we find each other, it's beautiful
> If not, it can't be helped.[12]

I remember the 'liberating' feel of this dictum — it seemed almost a high ideal, and it *was* in part a reaction against a world in which you made your bed and laid on it. But with hindsight the instruction to 'move on' had very little to do with feminism whose mainspring was a realisation of the oppression of women and the need for collective struggle. We might have come to this realisation through a wish to determine our own lives, but the debate was not about how we could use each other as long as it served our purposes, but how we could learn from and support each other. The goal of individual fulfilment must have been particularly confusing to mothers (many of whom did feel abandoned in the early days of the women's movement). What does it mean to 'put yourself first' with a baby? You can hardly 'move on' from children. Indeed, the 'marketplace psychology' of the 1960s and 1970s, which contained a deep confusion between self-respect and self-devotion, has set up many conflicting feelings. If you are *supposed* to put yourself first, how come you are desperately short of sleep and wandering around in a daze? Is there a difference between giving and self-sacrifice? Or not? Wrong for me but not wrong for the children? If wrong for me, then wrong for the children too? Or not? How can she stay at home like that? How can she go out to work like that?

All close relationships involve ambivalence and compromise, but the ethic of self-fulfilment seemed to be aimed at abolishing such problems. And if, as far as mothers and children were concerned, the problems just wouldn't go away the marketplace psychologists were quite prepared to abandon them. In *Winners and Losers: the Art of Self-Image Modification*, published in 1974, the authors wrote:

> If men are better off in any area of divorce, it's because they choose to be better off; if women are worse off, it's because they've chosen to be worse off. As for freedom from children, the best way to be free from children is not to conceive them . . .[13]

Women who have children must take the consequences.

Looking back at these different child-raising theories and the different tasks assigned to mothers, it is easy to take a critical view – forgetting that not so long ago they may have been just as much a part of our own thinking. How about the not-so-distant frenzy to educate our children while still in the cradle – the hanging of flashcards around the nursery so that baby may be well on the way to reading before he/she can even speak? Or Penelope Leach's exhortation just to have *fun* with your child – how come this innocent goal seems to slip so often between our fingers? No doubt we are just as avid now for anything that will tell us how to be a good mother. Indeed, we can learn an enormous amount from other people's understanding of babies and children. How can we disentangle it all?

There seems to be a crucial difference between two types

of theories. On the one hand, there are those which start from a particular definition of what it means to be a mother and on this basis lay down a particular prescription for motherhood. The mother is made responsible – both in the sense that she must carry out certain functions in order to meet certain needs in the child, and in the sense that in order to fulfil these functions she must herself be, unconsciously as well as consciously, a certain kind of person. On the other hand, there are those theories which do not start from a particular position in order to impart advice and educate, but reflect upon the dilemma of being a mother.

Psychoanalysis might always seem to make the mother responsible, but there is a fundamental difference between those theoretical positions that see the child in terms of certain universal needs that it is within the power of the mother to fulfil; and 'those theories like Freud's which have always avoided this precisely by demonstrating that the level of psychical life is not the same as the level of reality at which a mother "manages" her child'.[14] The level of social reality is that at which we consciously relate to our children, trying to do the best for them that we can. The level of psychic reality involves everything that is unconscious and eludes our control and yet plays an enormously powerful part in the relationship.

These two levels – the social and the psychic – do not coincide, indeed they are for the main part in conflict, because of the opposition between conscious and unconscious mind. For it is into the unconscious that we repress all those thoughts, feelings and impulses that it would be too painful or unacceptable to admit to conscious awareness. These feelings find expression in dreams, slips of the tongue or a whole pattern of living, but always in a disguised and unreadable form since if there is pressure for them to find expression, there is an equal pressure for them not to be known. The important point is that there are major parts of our mind that we have no knowledge of and that are outside our conscious control. To say that a mother has it in her

185

power to make herself fully responsible for the psychic health of her child seems therefore to deny the existence of the unconscious, both her own and that of the child.

The unconscious is an elusive idea. How can one credit something which by definition one can never really know about? Perhaps it is everything that we vaguely know about ourselves but would rather not think about? In fact, unconscious means literally unconscious, no matter how difficult it might be to believe that there is a part of ourselves, indeed the greater part, that consciously we know nothing about, except in so far as it reveals itself in a fleeting, random and often incomprehensible way.

The timelessness of the unconscious means that what happened thirty years ago is as immediate, in the unconscious, as what happened yesterday, however blurred or absent it may be in conscious memory. It is this that makes having a baby such a powerful event. Childbirth brings all sorts of pressures – lack of sleep, anxiety about the baby's welfare; frequently, in our society, isolation. But somehow this does not account for the fact that although we may have spent months preparing, consciously and unconsciously, for the idea of having a baby, it often comes as a shock. We never realised we'd feel so strongly. This is because the baby speaks to our unconscious selves where our own lives and feelings as infants are as present as our contemporary lives. We feel a baby's anger, comfort, fear of disintegration or bliss almost as though it were our own – not because our own feelings are a mirror image of the baby's, but because we too have been, and still are at a certain unconscious level, an infant ourselves. Our feelings as infants can be rearoused at any time, but they are particularly strongly called forth by caring for a totally dependent infant who was until recently actually 'part of' ourselves. It is this that makes mothers (and others who look after young children) so sensitive to their baby's feelings – what distresses the baby distresses the mother; and what satisfies the baby is deeply satisfying to the infant in the mother.

I have said that there is a crucial difference between the conscious social level at which we relate to our children, and our unconscious relationship with them, so much of which eludes our conscious understanding and control. All psychoanalysis takes as its base this opposition between conscious and unconscious mind. However, when an account of mothers and children is given in terms of a child's needs and its mother's task in fulfilling them, the opposition between the two seems to fade. It is not that a baby or child does not have crucial needs which if left unanswered may lead to real deprivation. But we are always talking about participants with their own history active in the present in a way that is largely unconscious.

Winnicott's term, the 'good enough' mother, has been greeted with a feeling of relief by many mothers; here at last is someone who will let us off being perfect. His writing about children has given me tremendous insight and reassurance. Nonetheless, there is also a sense in which the figure of the 'good enough' mother 'beckons merely to ensnare the real mother',[15] since it still involves the fulfilling of needs. Winnicott is opposed to mothers being given rules and regulations. His aim in writing for mothers is not to tell them what to do, but 'to give them the real and right reasons for their good intuitive feelings',[16] 'to put into words what a mother does when she is ordinarily and quite simply devoted to her baby.'[17] But his words, in part because they are so compelling, and in part because they are framed within a climate of maternal success or failure, amount to a powerful body of advice: they 'define, albeit in general terms, the path the good mother takes'.[18] Starting from what the baby needs, his advice is to follow 'your good intuitive feelings', to be 'natural': 'the baby needs just exactly what a mother does well if she is easy, natural, and lost in the job'.[19] But can a mother be defined in terms of what the baby needs? It sounds so simple, but we can get very entangled in the idea of 'natural'. Winnicott has a very precise definition of the word: a 'natural' mother has an instinctive, intuitive understanding of her child's needs. But what if the unconscious, on which she draws so much for this intuitive understanding, not only facilitates but also obstructs this understanding? And to what extent can she make use of 'information' to be a better kind of intuitive mother when access to a large part of what determines her feelings is not open to her? Supposing she is not an 'easy' kind of person, however much she loves her baby? Supposing she is at times actually *lost* in the job? How far does telling her not to be anxious create in her an ability to be 'calmly and consistently continuing to act naturally'? 'Good enough mother?'[20] said a friend, 'Fine, if you feel a good enough mother.'

In order to expand a bit more on what it means to talk about motherhood in terms of a baby's needs, let us look at Winnicott's description of the young baby and mother. He writes that in the beginning, the first few weeks of life, 'there is no such thing as a baby', only a 'nursing couple'[21]: 'If you set out to describe a baby, you will find you are describing a *baby and someone*. A baby cannot exist alone, but is essentially part of a relationship.'[22] By this he means that the child is totally dependent on its mother not only for its physical survival but also for any sense of psychic continuity. The mother, in his view, provides a sense of 'going-on-being' through her 'holding' of the infant – in part supplying essential physical care, but fundamentally through a 'form of loving' in which whatever she is doing she intuitively adapts herself to the constantly changing needs of the child. As long as the baby is held by the mother in this way it takes its 'going-on-being' for granted, unnoticed, like the air it breathes. Should the mother, however, fail seriously in this loving attention, causing a break beyond a point that is bearable to that child, the baby experiences unbearable anxiety tantamount to feeling a threat of annihilation. An extreme result of repeated breaks of this kind might be a baby who, for no apparent physical reason, 'fails to thrive'.

In Winnicott's view, such 'good-enough' mothering is

not a matter of 'intellectual understanding of the baby's needs'. It springs from a very special state of identification of the mother with the child, a state which he describes as 'primary maternal preoccupation' – a state of 'heightened sensitivity, almost an illness' in which the mother can 'feel herself into her infant's place, and so meet the infant's need.' He speaks of 'an almost magical understanding of need'.[23]

As time passes, the merger between mother and child begins to lessen. The baby begins to acquire some sense of self, some kind of distinction between itself and the rest of the world, a possibility of separateness between itself and its mother. As this happens, the need for the mother to be so finely attuned to her child begins to recede. Indeed, it is important, according to Winnicott, that the mother should gradually and progessively fail in her minute adaptation to the child, adapting, by *not* adapting, to its growing ability to have a separate sense of self and make its own 'signals' of need, as from one being to another. If she goes on being a 'magical' mother who knows what the child wants almost before it does, she is in danger of becoming a 'witch'.

Where the good-enough mother is able to provide this 'almost magical understanding of need', Winnicott's portrait of mother and child, has a relatively quiet feeling, the infant lies more or less peaceful in its union with mother. Bion gives a more dramatic description of the interactions between child and mother, both at this early stage and later. He describes the way in which the infant attempts to rid itself of terrifying unconscious phantasies – terror of disintegration, overwhelming rage or grief – by projecting them out on to the mother. The task of the mother is to take in her infant's distress, to bear the pain, to act if possible to alleviate it, at the very least to 'know about' it in some conscious or unconscious way and to feed back to the child the possibility that the distress is *thinkable about* and can be contained. The unthinkable-about feelings of the child are thus reworked by the mother and fed back by her to the child in a tolerable form – 'Oh dear, did you get squashed on your side and couldn't see where Mummy was!' It makes no difference that the baby does not yet understand language – it nonetheless receives a communication that disaster is no longer disaster. In Bion's words, the unbearable anxiety of the child

> shows itself as behaviour reasonably calculated to arouse in the mother feelings of which the infant wishes to be rid. If the infant feels that it is dying it can arouse fears that it is dying in the mother. A well-balanced mother can accept these and respond therapeutically; that is to say in a manner that makes the infant feel it is receiving its frightened personality back again but in a form that it can tolerate – the fears are manageable by the infant personality.[24]

If the mother cannot accept this projection, the baby 'reintrojects, not a fear of dying made tolerable, but a nameless dread'.[25]

This is a very vivid picture of how the baby causes the mother to feel its feelings. In case it is not immediately recognisable, think of a baby screaming somewhere in a supermarket, the pressing desire one has to see if everything is 'all right', our relief when the mother consoles the child – you can even then smile at other people in the queue, we all knew how we felt. Imagine a cry that went out into the universe for ever. . . .

However, in both these writers, and in much writing about mothers and children, the analytic detail seems to be focused mainly on the experience of the child and the mother's function in responding to it, on an expectation of mothering rather than the mother's experience. Given the lasting effect of early childhood experiences, it is vital that we should understand what it is that the baby most needs and how things can go right or wrong. However, the portrait of the mother given by this kind of writing seems curiously flat compared with the intense and ambivalent feelings which many mothers experience in having a child (not only a first tiny infant but older children as well). When we hear of the mother who intuitively knows what to do for her child, what its 'needs' are, of the 'well-balanced' mother who is able to 'respond therapeutically', it somehow leaves out of the account the turmoil and sense of not-knowing that many of us have been through, whatever our love for our children.

The view we have looked at so far talks of infant *needs* and maternal *functions* – what the baby needs and how the mother can fulfil these needs. For Freud, on the other hand, the mother is primarily the love object of the child, the focus of its passionate libidinal desires. There is no way, however, in which the mother can fully satisfy these desires – the child's love for her is by definition insatiable. Freud writes:

> Childhood love is boundless; it demands exclusive possession, it is not content with less than all. But it has a second characteristic: it has, in point of fact, no aim and is incapable of obtaining complete satisfaction; and principally for that reason it is doomed to end in disappointment and to give place to a hostile attitude.[26]

'Not content with less than all' – the child's love demands total capture of the mother but by this token contains the ever-present possibility of loss, in phantasy as well as actuality: the breast that comes and goes, the inevitable rival claims of father and siblings.

'No sexual aim' – unlike an adult whose sexual drives are constructed to a point of seeking expression in a certain direction, the drives of a child are always in the process of construction. Childhood sexuality exists, but though there may be a sense of sensual bliss, satisfaction is not possible in the same way.

'A hostile attitude' – however caring the mother in real

life, she will always be held responsible for the loss that psychically she represents to the child. The mother, whatever her variety of mothering, is structurally bound to disappoint, to be a 'cruel' mother.

What we are talking about here is clearly not manageable love between child and mother but impossible passions. Whether or not you feel at home with such a powerfully drawn picture of the human condition, there is no doubt that there is an intense crossplay of the unconscious life of both mother and child – for just as the child makes impossible demands on its mother, so 'the child cannot escape the play of the mother's psychic life across its own'.[27] It is this which makes for the texture and quality of emotional life, for good or for bad. Simone de Beauvoir writes of her childhood:

> I recall the surprise we felt when, after asking Mama if we might take our dolls on holiday with us, she answered simply: 'Why not?' We had repressed this wish for years. Certainly the main reason for my timidity was a desire to avoid her derision. But at the same time, whenever her eyes had that stormy look or even when she just compressed her lips, I believe that I feared the disturbance I was causing in her heart more than my own discomfiture. If she had found me out telling a lie, I should have felt the scandal it created even more keenly than any personal shame: but the idea was so unbearable, I always told the truth. I obviously did not realise that my mother's promptness to condemn anything peculiar or new was a forestalling of the confusion that any dispute aroused in her: but I sensed that careless words and sudden changes of plan easily troubled her serenity. My responsibility towards her made my dependence even greater. That is how we lived, the two of us, in a kind of symbiosis.[28]

There is nothing unusual in saying that the relationship

between mother and child exists on unconscious as well as conscious levels. However, these are two different and conflicting levels – the practical level of reality at which the mother cares for her child is not the same as the level of unconscious life, nor do they run in tandem. To set up any normative standard of mothering, to tell her that to be a good mother she must be like this or like that with her child, is to deny the existence of this conflict, to imply that the unconscious is something that can be brought under control and be got to behave reasonably and rationally. To me such a standard would seem to deny the existence of the unconscious. According to this normative scheme of things, the mother is innately and biologically fitted to care for her child because of her experience of carrying it through pregnancy; the infant's impossible desires become 'needs' that can with care be satisfied; the mother's unconscious, ambivalent feelings become a state of extraordinary sensitivity which allow her to meet these needs with an even closer match than would otherwise be possible; in her 'holding' of the psychic environment she lends the infant the support of her own stable self and steady relation to reality for as long as its own frail sense of self and safety require.

But this view of the interaction between mother and child puts forward a picture of coherence and stability in our relationship to reality that some writers would question. Freud speaks of the impossibility of the infant's desires. He also sees our relationship as adults to reality as inevitably problematic: not only because of the impossibility of unconscious life ever coinciding with the social order, but also because of the unremitting conflict between the two.

Jacques Lacan, following on from Freud, sees the human subject as one who has essentially lost something, is in search of something, right from the beginning, even before the breast that comes and goes. That which we have lost, a sense of perfection and wholeness, is that which we desire and can never find – we find only the illusion of unity. A

193

powerful image for him of this illusory unity is the gap between an infant's physical and psychic discoordination (he may not be able to stand upright, let alone manage his thoughts) and the impression of unity and autonomy that he receives when he first recognises his image in a mirror: Look, there's me, all in one piece! Because of the split nature of the subject, the mother, though she can satisfy needs, can never be a source of final satisfaction.

> The mother's love cannot be absolute as she cannot fulfil this absolute *demand* for love made by the infant. No matter how much she gives him and how much his *needs* are satisfied, the mother can never fill the void she shares with her child. She is never perfect. The demand for love goes *beyond* the objects that satisfy need. In Lacan's view it is in this irreducible 'beyond' of demand that desire is constituted.[29]

Lacan's concept of desire as something that remains beyond fulfilment whatever the environment, something that cannot be managed, has been elaborated by writers such as Juliet Mitchell and Jacqueline Rose,[30] as well as other French psychoanalytic writers. For our purposes here, it is important to state that for Lacan the child's desire isn't synonymous with its desire for its mother. The love object of the child is an internalisation that the child constructs out of the mother and other elements of its experience, including always its own internal phantasies. And, as the above quotation makes clear, the lack from which desire springs is something that the mother shares with her child, so that the child can never in this sense be the final fulfilment of the mother either, however much for many women maternity might seem to be that which will finally 'complete' them.

Freud's picture of love doomed to end in disappointment may seem hard to live with and some revisers of Freud have sought to ameliorate the situation by reducing psychic conflict to social causes. Of course, they say, there are inevitable conflicts in childhood, but any major difficulties experienced in passing through them are really due to lack of understanding parents and a happy home. They decline to see human behaviour as one of enduring conflict between irreconcilable forces, and childhood miseries as inescapable, whatever the 'happy home'. Philip Rieff gives an account of Freud's view of family life which may seem extreme, but which attempts to combat the 'cheery platitudes' of Freud's revisers.

> Experience begins with a trauma, birth, and the child's unwonted separation from the mother; brothers and sisters do not welcome the newcomer, and there is a chance its parents, consciously or unconsciously, did not want the child either. How constricting, as well as protecting, is the family circle around the child. All family relations are competitive: the children are originally bound by mutual hatred, which is only later repudiated as a sacrifice to parental love. 'Being in love with one parent and hating the other' forms part of the permanent 'stock of psychical impulses' which arise in childhood early. The child lives in a world of frustration, goaded by unappeasable desires and envies. Childhood neuroses, Freud tells us, 'is not the exception but the rule'; it is 'unavoidable'.[31]

Bleak though this may seem, and perhaps over-intense in its distillation, it is through the dynamic of such conflict – the endless moving backwards and forwards – that we are able to grow and develop, though the process is never at an end. (We should also remember that these are largely repressed unconscious conflicts, hence the rather 'shocking' impact of this portrait.)

There is, however, a very powerful pull towards denying conflict, uncertainty and loss, because of the pain of not being finally consoled. And it is women, as objects of love or of hate, who become the most powerful repository for the wish for everything to be made better, both because of their psychic continuity with the figure of Mother, and because by and large it is they who do actually mother. It is not only that they are somehow to compensate everyone else for the ills of the world, but that they themselves are placed in a position where there is the greatest possible illusion of a possibility for total love – the dream couple of mother and child. Penelope Leach writes, in *Baby and Child*,

> You are going to know this person better than you will ever know anybody else. Nobody else in the world including your partner, however devoted, is ever going to love you as much as he will in these first years if you will let him. You are into a relationship which is unique and which can be uniquely rewarding.[32]

I am acutely aware of the intensity of feeling of mother for child and child for mother, but I think it is very important not to idealise motherhood – namely, to see a possibility for perfect bliss between mother and child, a relationship in which mother has it in her power to make everything all right. There are many moments of bliss – the baby falls blissfully asleep at the breast; and long stretches of ordinary contentment. Equally, however, human behaviour is essentially one of ambivalent emotions and conflict. It is one thing to struggle to meet our child's needs better than we do, or to feel the discomfort of not being able to meet demands that go beyond the possibility of fulfilment, but quite another to see only our own guilt in any failure of bliss, any powerfully mixed feelings, any intractable conflict for the child or ourselves.

Guilt is all the more powerful because of the burden of responsibility that is put on mothers. We have seen how ever-changing ideals of motherhood are set up by society as a means of regulating mothers and through them family life. When the message to mothers is at its most crude it is still powerful. I am thinking here of the present campaign of

196

the Right to fasten responsibility for the current 'moral decline' of the country on the churches, teachers and parents, meaning ultimately mothers. Neal Ascherson questions this view: '... there is something hollow about Mr Hurd's call for police and teachers and Churches and families. There is, I suspect, one other question which he felt it prudent not to ask. Where are the mothers?'[33] It is they who, according to the new moralists, are supposed to provide the stability in the home which should lead to harmony and social cohesion in society as a whole – except that for Mr Hurd social cohesion has more to do with law and order than with social unity born of greater social equality. And there is something about law and order that is aligned with 'traditional' values (everyone knowing their place and not complaining about it) as opposed to feminism's questioning of sexual politics. Isabella MacKay, daughter of David Stayt, founder of Concern for Family and Womanhood, recently told *Cosmopolitan* magazine, 'Feminism is responsible for the rising divorce rate, abortion, child-molesting and also rape. Society encourages women to seek divorce; children are generally molested because their mothers don't look after them properly.'[34] Political problems and issues are thus transformed into a political strategy to censure moral failings in the family, i.e. the mother. All this happens at a time of increasing abandonment of state commitment to mothers and children: the Conservative Government has reduced women's entitlement to maternity leave, pay and rights; introduced taxation on workplace nurseries; reduced nursery education and pre-school childcare; restricted the right of unemployed married women to register for work; frozen child benefit; shifted entitlement to social security benefits in the direction of family means testing, thus increasing women's financial dependence on men.

What all coercive definitions of motherhood have in common is a way of presenting what it means to be a mother as something pregiven and innate – mothers may

vary over time and place, but there is something inescapa-
bly 'eternal' about mothering. The recourse to Nature, plus
our own longings for certainty and oneness, give enormous
normative power to any particular prescription for
motherhood – nature has ordained, there can be no questioning. Indeed, questioning is often seen as corrupting. A
recent article in *Practical Parenting* entitled, 'Are you a born
mother?', states:

> The trouble is that women's emancipation/liberation, call
> it what you will, has come full circle. We've fought
> bitterly for the right to use our brains and then we feel
> guilty when we suddenly relinquish our grey cells on the
> day we give birth and are forced to adjust to the mind of a
> child. It's not only hard for career women. Degrees can
> never transform them into vocational mothers who ask
> for nothing out of life but child-rearing. It's also hard for
> any woman who finds it a shock to have to put number
> one into second place.[35]

In this article the author 'investigates motherhood, talking
to some of those who know the secret and others who'd like
to' – i.e. there is something called 'motherhood' in which
the reader can be instructed.

A Freudian view, on the other hand, sees motherhood
(and related identities such as what it means to be a man, a
woman, a child) as an ever-shifting construction. There is
nothing given or innate, rather we are formed and constantly reformed through our own conscious and unconscious histories and what comes to us from the world
around us. Lacan, as we have seen, sees the human subject
as something marked by lack right from the beginning. It is
through our attempts to live with conflict, to make an
ever-changing meaning of it, that we construct what it
means to us to be a mother, and that meaning is never final,
always precarious and changing. There is no set thing
about being a mother. Every woman who has a baby (or has

no baby) has phantasies, conscious and unconscious, of how she will feel, what the baby will be like, what they will mean to each other. If these are not borne out in reality, she has to make readjustments to cope with the resulting internal conflict, until further disjunctions arise to cause further readjustment.

Balzac's novel, *Memoirs of Two Young Married Women*,[36] gives a very vivid picture of the way in which one mother's conscious ideas and unconscious phantasies of what it means to be a mother shift and change in line with her inner life and the ideas she has received and made her own from the society in which she lives. Balzac, who in his novels set out to catalogue French nineteenth-century life, based his portrait of this woman on conversations he had with a woman friend, Zulma Carraud. Renée de l'Estorade, the heroine of the novel, sees maternity as a final and blissful consolation for something intangible that she craves. Writing to her friend, Madame de Macumer, she says,

> I desire to be a mother – if only to give food to the craving activity of my soul . . . Maternity is an enterprise in which I have opened an enormous stake . . . Motherhood will develop my energy, enlarge my heart, and compensate me for all things by infinite joys!

But her phantasies about what maternity will accomplish for her come up against obstacles in reality. She had expected the biological fact of being pregnant to produce a blissful maternal response in her. When she feels 'nothing', she is deeply shamed and has to resign herself to the shifting imaginings of her mind rather than what she had thought would be the unequivocal messages of her body. She writes to her friend:

> . . . they talk to me of the happiness of being a mother. Alas! I alone feel nothing; I dare not tell you the state of absolute insensibility in which I find myself. I fib a little,

199

so as not to sadden their joy. But I may speak honestly to you, and I must admit that so far as I have gone, maternity begins in the imagination.

She is equally aghast when she is shown the new-born baby – he is not what she had dreamt of:

My dear, I was horrified!
'That little monkey!' I cried. 'Are you sure it is a child!'

It is the erotic experience of the baby at her breast, tinged with some pleasure in pain, that finally matches her fantasy of motherhood:

The little monster took my breast and sucked: There, there was the *fiat lux*! Suddenly I was a mother. Here is happiness, and here is joy, ineffable joy – though not without some pain.

But this also shifts, or is built upon. The difficulties of caring for a young baby produce in Renée a notion of motherhood as one of tireless and minute devotion.

The science of motherhood carries with it many a silent merit, unknown to all others and without parallel – virtue in small things, devotion at all hours. I must watch over the soup. You don't think me a woman to withhold myself from a single care, do you? Why should I leave to another woman the care and pleasure of blowing on a spoonful of soup which Naïs may find too hot . . .?

Renée's anxious, devotional care is in part her response to the vulnerability of a tiny child, and in part reflects the nineteenth-century ideal of femininity and motherhood as a holy office. There was already a flavour of 'resignation and devotion' when she first married an ailing man twenty years her senior and gave herself to him 'just as a mother (according to my ideas of what a mother should be) exhausts herself in her attempt to bring pleasure to her child.' Nonetheless, we see in this account how Renée creates and recreates her own meaning of motherhood–both from what comes to her from the outside world and from her own inner phantasies: maternity indeed exists in the imagination. (Of course this is Balzac's novel in which he gives expression to his own construction of women and mothers, and possibly, through the emotional engagement of the novel, causes a shift in that of the reader's.)

As mothers we are involved in passions that make us both powerful and vulnerable – powerful because of the strength of our love for our children, vulnerable because of the intensity of the feelings that they stir up in us. It is because we love that we can hate. Or even because we hate that we can love. We draw on all the emotional resources of our unconscious lives without necessarily knowing what is taking place. There is always a gap between our phantasy of motherhood and our actual experience of it, a dissonance between conscious 'knowing' and the unconscious.

In the face of this conflict advice becomes very important to us. We want it and use it, and can be very comforted by it. But advice also contains many ambiguities and dangers. Firstly, it tends to embody everything that mothers come to stand for to the rest of the world (of which we form part). We can be buffeted and disorientated by what is set up as good, bad, success or failure. (Moreover, ideals of motherhood are not necessarily matched by social commitment to the material security of mothers and children – families with children are presently the fastest growing group amongst the poor.) Secondly, because of the gap between external reality and the imagination, advice – whether a particular course of action or a way of being – may be precisely that which we cannot follow.

The women's movement has always drawn its strength from experience rather than edict. Hearing the unspoken spoken has given us enormous support. However, not everything can be spoken. We still come up against the intractable repetition of unconscious patterns, the split between what is known and what is not known. To deny this conflict, to seek safety in prescription, is to be merely defensive, to stop ourselves from hearing what we might have come to hear. To allow ourselves some attentiveness to conflict is the beginning of using it creatively. Mothers may be born in the imagination and we may be almost too close to them to see them. But perhaps this book will bring them into a stronger relief.

Notes

1. Jacques Donzelot, *The Policing of Families*, Hutchinson, 1980.
2. Barbara Ehrenreich and Deirdre English, *For Her Own Good: 150 Years of the Experts' Advice to Women*, Pluto Press, 1979.
3. John B. Watson, *Psychological Care of Infant and Child*, W. W. Norton, 1928, pp. 81–2.
4. Frances L. Ilg and Louise Bates Ames, *Child Behaviour*, Harper & Row, 1951, p. 64.
5. Ehrenreich and English, op. cit., p. 198.
6. Ehrenreich and English, op. cit., p. 203.
7. Ehrenreich and English, op. cit., p. 204.
8. Betty Friedan, *The Feminine Mystique*, W. W. Norton, 1963, p. 191.
9. Ehrenreich and English, op. cit., p. 234.
10. Ehrenreich and English, op. cit., p. 250.
11. Ehrenreich and English, op. cit., p. 253.
12. Fritz Perls and John O. Stevens, *Gestalt Therapy Verbatim*, California; Real People Press, 1969, p. 4.
13. Howard M. Newberger and Marjorie Lee, *Winners and Losers: The Art of Self-Image Modification*, New York: David McKay, 1974, p. 25.
14. Parveen Adams, 'Mothering, *m/f*, No. 8, 1983, p. 40. I am greatly indebted to this paper in writing this chapter.
15. Adams, op. cit., p. 44.
16. D. W. Winnicott, *The Child, the Family and the Outside World*, Penguin Books, 1964, p. 176.
17. Winnicott, op. cit., p. 18.

18. Adams, op. cit., p. 44.
19. Winnicott, op. cit., p. 27.
20. Winnicott, op. cit., p. 129.
21. D. W. Winnicott, *Through Paediatrics to Psycho-Analysis*, Hogarth Press, 1982, p. 99.
22. Winnicott, *The Child, the Family and the Outside World*, p. 88.
23. Winnicott, *The Maturational Processes and the Facilitating Environment*, Hogarth Press, 1985, p. 50.
24. W. R. Bion, *Second Thoughts: Selected Papers on Psycho-Analysis*, Maresfield Reprints, 1984, p. 114.
25. *Ibid.*, p. 116.
26. Sigmund Freud, *On Sexuality*, Pelican Freud Library, 1977, p. 378.
27. Adams, op. cit., p. 42.
28. Simone de Beauvoir, *Memoirs of a Dutiful Daughter*, Penguin Books, 1963, pp. 40–1.
29. Bice Benvenuto and Roger Kennedy, *The Works of Jacques Lacan, An Introduction*, St Martin's Press, 1986, p. 174.
30. For example, Juliet Mitchell and Jacqueline Rose (eds.), *Feminine Sexuality, Jacques Lacan and the École Freudienne*, Macmillan, 1982.
31. Philip Rieff, *Freud: The Mind of the Moralist*, University of Chicago Press, 1959, third edition 1979, p. 57.
32. Penelope Leach, *Baby and Child, From Birth to Age Five*, Penguin Books, 1977, p. 21.
33. Neal Ascherson, 'Why the English lost cohesion', *Observer*, 20 March 1988.
34. Isabella MacKay, 'Where on Earth is a Woman's Place?', *Cosmopolitan*, February 1988.
35. Jane Bidder, 'Are You a Born Mother?', *Practical Parenting*, A Family Circle Publication, July 1988.
36. Honoré de Balzac, *Memoirs of Two Young Married Women*, first published 1842.

Biographies

Helena Kennedy was born in Glasgow in 1950. She was called to the English Bar in 1972 and has practised at the Bar for sixteen years. She has written on the Bar, on legal issues, on violence against women, and on child sexual abuse. Throughout 1987 she presented BBC's 'Heart of the Matter' and is an occasional presenter of 'After Dark' on Channel Four. She is working on a book about women and crime and has just created a drama series for BBC 2 called 'Blind Justice'.

Elizabeth Wilson is a writer and teacher who lives in London. She began adult life as an aesthete, became involved in feminist and left politics in the 1970s, and still strives for a politics of progressive decadence.

Yasmin Alibhai was born in Uganda where she lived until she was twenty-three. After completing her BA degree in literature at Makerere University, Uganda, she came to Britain and went to Oxford where she did her M.Phil. in literature and society. She taught English for several years, and then joined the Inner London Education Authority as a lecturer in equal opportunities. Since 1984, she has been a print and radio journalist, writing mainly on race issues. She has produced programmes for Capital Radio and the

BBC and has written for the *Guardian*, *London Daily News*, *Nursing Times*, *Asian Times*, *New Society*, etc. She is currently on the *New Statesman and Society*. She has a ten-year-old son, Ari.

Katherine Gieve, born in 1949, is a solicitor specialising in children's law. She is co-author of *The Cohabitation Handbook*, a women's guide to the law (Pluto Press), and writes freelance on both feminism and the law. She lives in London with her husband and their two children aged eight and six.

Victoria Hardie was born in England, raised in Kent then London, and educated in Salisbury, Wiltshire until the age of seventeen. She wrote without payment in between jobs as a photographic model, messenger girl, shop assistant; getting married, moving to Herefordshire and becoming a mother. During the last decade she became a professional writer. Her play *The Perfect Wife* was performed at the Bush Theatre, *Toy Boy* at the Riverside Studios, *Us Good Girls* at the Soho Poly and *Vital Statistics*, an opera composed by Michael Nyman and the artist Paul Richards. She has since moved back to London and is working on a commission for the Royal Court Theatre Upstairs and on a short story for Anthony Blond, the publisher. She is married and has two sons aged eleven and five years old.

Hilary Land is a professor of Social Policy at Royal Holloway and Bedford New College, University of London. She was educated at West Suffolk County Grammar School, Bristol University and LSE. Her first piece of research in the 1960s was a study of large families from which grew an interest in family resources and family allowances in particular. This broadened into an interest in State policies and the family at the same time as the re-emergence of the women's movement. She was a member of the Women's Liberation Fifth Demand Group and the YBA Wife Campaign in the 1970s. She has written numerous articles on women and the Welfare State, distribution of resources within the family and more recently women's work and women's time. Her daughter, Dienka, was born on New Year's Day 1980.

Rahila Gupta lived most of her life in India; she came to London in 1975. She has, for several years now, been active in various campaigns on women's issues, and is on the editorial of *Outwrite* women's newspaper. Two anthologies to which she contributed were published in 1988: *Charting the Journey* (Sheba), a collection of writings by black and Third World women: and *Right of Way* (Women's Press), creative writings from the Asian Women's Collective.

Elizabeth Peretz was born in 1948 in Nottinghamshire. Mother, teacher, researcher, friend, she currently lives near Oxford with children Jack, eleven and Ruth, nine. She was married in 1976 and divorced in 1987. She is a research assistant in the History of Medicine: her current work is on mothers' health and welfare in inter-war Britain.

Gillian Darley is a freelance journalist and photographer, specialising in architecture. She has also published four books and is currently completing a biography of Octavia Hill. Her husband is a barrister and they live in Holborn. Joseph Horowitz was born on 18 January 1987 and died on 3 April 1987.

Jean Radford teaches literature and cultural studies in a polytechnic. She has two children, aged eight and a half and two and a half, and lives in London with them and their father.

Jennifer Uglow was born in 1947. She is now principal editor at the Hogarth Press. She has written several introductions to Virago Victorians and to the *Virago Book of Ghost Stories*. Her books include *The Macmillan Biographic Dictionary of Women* (2nd ed. Spring 1989) and the Virago Pioneer *George Eliot*. She is currently working on a biography of Mrs Gaskell. She was married in 1971 to Steve Uglow, senior lecturer in Law at the University of Kent; they have four children.

Margaret Smith trained as a reporter in her home town of Barnstaple, after graduating from the University of Exeter. Three children (Andrew, Patrick and Ellen) later, she and her husband Geoff moved to Oxford where he is a lecturer at Westminster College. Daughter Emma arrived in 1970. After 12 years of largely unpaid motherhood, Margaret Smith became local government correspondent for the *Oxford Mail and Times* and is now deputy news editor there. The family now live a relatively uneventful life in the market town of Witney, trying to keep abreast of housework, gardening and decorating, but preferring hillwalking, sport, reading, doing crosswords and good company, conversation and malt whisky at their local.

Julia Vellacott has two children and works as a psychotherapist in North London.

OTHER VIRAGO BOOKS OF INTEREST

THE MOTHER KNOT
Jane Lazarre

'Beautifully written . . . *The Mother Knot* says the unsayable, crackling with insights . . . Jane Lazarre ventures where no mother has ever ventured except under cover of fiction. At once profoundly consoling and terrifying, her finds are universal' — *Washington Post Book World*

In this honest and moving book Jane Lazarre explores her own experiences of motherhood — the joy of feeling her baby move inside her, the pain and wonder of giving birth, the exhaustion of caring for a demanding newborn, the transformation of her identity, and her conflicting feelings of pleasure, fear, helplessness, love and guilt. Interweaving glimpses of daily life with internal reflections, she vividly captures the first few years of motherhood, the transition from the earliest days to the moment when her child attends a creche and she is able to pursue other commitments. Always there is ambivalence: she longs for escape to regain her lost independence, but she longs just as fiercely for total immersion in her infant. Lively, often very funny, altogether absorbing, this is an intensely personal tale which also reaches out to embrace experiences that all mothers share, raising such crucial issues as shared parenting, conceptions of the self and women's work.

IN MY MOTHER'S HOUSE
A daughter's story

Kim Chernin

'So, do you want to take down the story of my life?' Rose Chernin demands of her daughter Kim when they meet after a long separation. In 1914 Rose and her mother had left Russia for the dream that was America. There the formidable Rose rebelled against the injustices she had not expected to meet, went to the Russian Club in New York, danced, discussed, debated. During the Depression she joined the Communist Party and in the early 1930s Rose and her husband went to Moscow, caught up in the excitement of that changing society. They returned to California and Rose travelled the country, speaking and organising fearlessly until she was jailed in the McCarthy era.

During these years Kim loved, resented and feared for her absent and notorious 'Red' mother, and, at seventeen, completely rejected her politics. But in writing down her mother's life and her own, they both came to understand that, 'We are not enemies, we are only a mother and a daughter. We see the world differently.'

FIERCE ATTACHMENTS
Vivian Gornick

'One hesitates to traffic in such stock reviewers' adjectives as "brilliant", "an American classic", but there are only so many words to say how very good this book is. *Fierce Attachments* deserves them all'

– *Washington Post*

In this gripping memoir, Vivian Gornick tells the story of her lifelong battle with her mother for independence. Born and raised in the Bronx, the daughter of Jewish immigrants, she grows up in a household dominated by her mercurial mother. Next door lives Nellie, a beautiful, red-haired Gentile, whose disturbing, sensual presence provides a powerful antidote to the sexual repression which underpins her mother's romantic myth-making. These women with their opposing models of 'femininity' continue, well into adulthood, to shape Vivian Gornick's struggle to define herself in love and in work.

Now in her middle years, she walks with her aged mother through the streets of New York, talking, arguing and remembering the past. Each is a wonderful raconteur, and as they tell and retell stories, they bring to life the dramas, characters and atmosphere of their tenement block. But what emerges from these evocations is yet another story – Vivian Gornick's unflinchingly honest account of an attachment that remains as fiercely loving and difficult today as it has been throughout her life.